THE HUNTERS
AND
THE HUNTED

*This is a volume in the
Arno Press Collection*

NAVIES AND MEN

*See last pages of this volume
for a complete list of titles.*

THE HUNTERS
AND
THE HUNTED

ALDO COCCHIA

Translated by M. Gwyer

ARNO PRESS
A New York Times Company
New York • 1980

Editorial Supervision: Erin Foley

Reprint Edition 1980 by Arno Press Inc.

Copyright © 1958 by United States Naval Institute

Reprinted by permission of Naval Institute Press

NAVIES AND MEN
ISBN for complete set: 0-405-13030-9
See last pages of this volume for titles.

Manufactured in the United States of America

Library of Congress Cataloging in Publication Data

Cocchia, Aldo, 1900-
   The hunters and the hunted.

   (Navies and men)
   Translation of Sommergibili all'attacco.
   Reprint of the ed. published by United States
Naval Institute, Annapolis, Md.
   1. World War, 1939-1945--Naval operations--
Submarine. 2. World War, 1939-1945--Naval
operations, Italian. I. Title. II. Series.
[D784.I8C6213 1980]   940.54'51   79-6106
ISBN 0-405-13035-X

THE HUNTERS
AND THE HUNTED

THE HUNTERS
AND
THE HUNTED

*Adventures of
Italian Naval Forces*

by

ADMIRAL ALDO COCCHIA

Translated by M. Gwyer

UNITED STATES NAVAL INSTITUTE
ANNAPOLIS, MARYLAND

First published in Great Britain under the title of "Submarine Attacking," by William Kimber and Co. Limited.

Copyright © 1958
BY
UNITED STATES NAVAL INSTITUTE
ANNAPOLIS, MD.

Library of Congress Catalogue No. 58-8018

PRINTED IN U.S.A.
BY
GEORGE BANTA CO., INC., MENASHA, WIS.

Contents

PART 1
OCEAN-GOING SUBMARINES

CHAPTER	PAGE
I. Commerce Raiding	1
II. Betasom	8
III. U-Boats	13
IV. Shift to the Atlantic	18
V. Salvatore Todaro, the Knight Errant	27
VI. Atlantic Incidents	34
VII. *Torelli's* Career	40
VIII. Pittoni and the *Bagnolini*	43
IX. Tramping to Singapore	47

PART 2
ADVENTURES IN UNIFORM

X. Invading Crete	59
XI. The Attack that Failed	70
XII. The *Kasbah*	77
XIII. Villa Carmela	81
XIV. The Ghost Ships	89

PART 3
CONVOYS

XV. The Battle of African Convoys	93
XVI. Blockade Runners	116
XVII. A Drama in Two Acts	122
XVIII. *Da Mosto's* Last Fight	127
XIX. Commander Ignazio Castrogiovanni	130

CHAPTER	PAGE
XX. Commander Enea Picchio	136

PART 4
FOUR BRAVE MEN

XXI. Admiral Carlo Bergamini	142
XXII. Carlo Fecia Di Cossato	149
XXIII. Human Torpedoes	156
XXIV. *Olterra's* Commander	172
Appendix: Italian Submarines in the Atlantic	179

List of Illustrations

Following page 24

Submarine night-attack against British convoy——Italian submarine cruising in the North Atlantic——Italian submarine entering Bordeaux docks.

Following page 56

Admiral Parona and the author (right) at Bordeaux——Admiral Doenitz inspects Italian crews at Bordeaux——An Italian submarine attacks a British tanker——Italian submarine *Malaspina* sinks *British Fame*——Armed merchantman torpedoed by Italian submarine——Italian submarine and U-boat meet on the high seas——Torpedo boat *Circe* sinks British submarine *Tempest*.

Following page 88

Makeshift landing-craft used in invasion of Crete——A convoy at Gibraltar. Villa Carmela in left center——*Vivaldi* runs into heavy weather while on convoy duty——"Ghost" ship, the light cruiser *Bartolomeo Colleoni* (Courtesy Lieut. Aldo Fraccaroli, INR)——*Monte Gargano* sinks after being hit by aerial torpedo——German steamer *Castellon* succumbs to torpedo attack——Convoy about to sail from Italian base in Adriatic——Typical Italian convoy en route to North Africa.

Following page 120

Infantry for Albania embarking on *Eugenio Di Savoia*——Loading German armored car on an Italian destroyer——Italian heavy cruiser during a night action——A cruiser of the *Zara* class in battle action——Three views of Italian "assault boat"——The dramatic Italian two-man torpedo or "pig."

Following page 152

"Pig" base in hold of *Olterra* at Algeciras, Spain——The submarine *Brin* which served during the entire war *(Courtesy Lieut. Aldo Fraccaroli, INR)*——A Mediterranean convoy workhorse, the *Da Recco (Courtesy Lieut. Aldo Fraccaroli, INR)*.

DIAGRAMS

Italian convoys' areas of operation 103
Cruises of the M.V. *Orseolo* 120
Plan for assault against Malta 166

Part 1. OCEAN-GOING SUBMARINES

I

Commerce Raiding

IT was the end of July 1940. One morning one of my submarines came into Spezia from the Atlantic and, as usual, I went down to greet her at the quay. When her Captain, Buonamici, came ashore, his first words were, of course, about his trip, which was of much interest as it was one of the first operations carried out by Italian submarines in the Atlantic. Then we went together to the Mess where a hearty meal was waiting—the kind of meal a man needs after forty days at sea. Just as we were going into the wardroom Buonamici made a remark which has stuck in my mind ever since. All he said was: "I must have some oranges." This casual remark seemed to epitomize better than a more elaborate speech the strain and privations of these long ocean cruises in which hazardous operations had to begin and end with a passage through the Straits of Gibraltar under the very eyes of the enemy.

No one wants to indulge in rhetoric; and it was precisely for that reason that I began this book in a minor key with the story of the oranges. But the fact remains that the adventures and achievements of the Italian Submarine Command during the war were far more extensive than is generally realized. I shall try to illustrate this later on by giving details of actual engagements and operations. For the moment we can concentrate on one point, namely that Italian submarines ran the gauntlet of the Strait of Gibraltar at least forty-four times with the loss of only one boat. Our single casualty was *Glauco* which was sunk on her homeward voyage in 1941, and she was not sunk in the Straits but on the surface, 250 miles farther west.

Since we are dealing with facts I must add something here by way of comparison. In the summer of 1941 twenty German U-boats were ordered into the Mediterranean from the Atlantic. They passed the Straits in the most favorable direction from a navigator's point of view and they had the benefit of all the advice and information that we could give them. None the less, the Germans lost five boats through sinkings. This is not said in criticism of the German commanders whose skill was beyond question; but it does give the measure of what was achieved by their Italian opposite numbers, who had to tackle the job as pioneers.

In the summer of 1940, the question was whether to attempt the passage on the surface or submerged. There was much to be said either way. Submerged one had the best chance, though hardly the certainty of avoiding British destroyers and corvettes. On the other hand, a strong current runs through the Straits from the Atlantic to the Mediterranean and one is bedevilled by cross-currents and eddies which always occur where two currents meet. There was some doubt whether the electric motors of a submerged submarine would be strong enough to make headway against it. From that point of view one was better off on the surface using diesels; but the operational arguments were all the other way.

This was the problem which plagued Submarine Command when, on orders from the Naval Staff, they were preparing to send our oceangoing submarines into the Atlantic. No one could say positively which was the right answer. In the end, it was decided that the known danger of enemy patrols was less serious than the unknown navigational risks of currents. Consequently, when the first submarine went through in June 1940,[1] her orders were to make the passage on the surface at night, after covering her approach by a series of elusive maneuvres between the Spanish and African shores.

An outsider—and I count myself as one, having never set foot in the Admiralty—might well ask why no trial submerged passage of the Straits was made before the war, since it was obvious even then that some of our larger submarines might one day have to operate in the Atlantic. I do not know the answer to that question. I can only say that the trial was *not* made, with the result that our submarines received the orders described above which left their captains no choice but to make the passage on the surface. In fact, they had to do so twice—once each way—because the Italian Atlantic Base at Bordeaux did not then exist and had not even been thought of.

The first two passages were made by *Finzi* and *Calvi*, both of the Spezia Group. They ran into no serious incidents, spent a month at sea and returned to base, having twice run the English lines successfully. The next to make the venture was *Cappellini*, then under Masi's command. She did not have such an easy time. Even at night someone was bound to stub his toe on the British sooner or later and it happened to be *Cappellini*. She nearly bumped into a destroyer and, since there was no time to dive, decided to fight it out on the surface. That night the Straits echoed with gunfire and the sea was furrowed by torpedoes on opposing tracks fired at close range. But, as often happens in unexpected night actions, neither ship was seriously damaged. *Cappellini*, however, having received some hits, broke off the engagement and ran for Ceuta. It was the best thing she could have done for, if the action had been prolonged, she

[1] Italy declared war on 11 June, 1940. (Tr.)

would certainly have been sunk. She remained at Ceuta for the twenty-four hours allowed by international law and then slipped out by night and returned to base.

The next submarine, *Veniero*, not only got through the Straits but established a precedent. Her captain—Buonamici of the oranges—decided that all the underwater boobytraps which nature had put at the bottom of the Straits were preferable to His Britannic Majesty's destroyers on the surface. So he blandly disregarded his orders, dived off Europa Point and made the passage submerged. He discovered that navigation, though difficult, was by no means impossible. He came safely through to the Atlantic, spent a month commerce-raiding, and then quietly re-entered the Mediterranean by the same method. His was the first submarine in the world to make this passage submerged in war time.

So far we had made six successful trips.

It was *Malaspina*'s turn next. She, too, made the passage submerged, without knowing at the time of *Veniero*'s success. But this time things were less easy. The natural boobytraps were in full operation and *Malaspina* had a pretty tough time. First she was caught in an eddy and made a sudden dive at an angle of thirty degrees down to 520 feet; then she was forced to the surface again only to go into a second dive heaven knows how deep. And all this, you must remember, within a few hundred yards of the main British base at Gibraltar. In fact, if *Malaspina*'s captain, Leoni, had not been one of the wiliest submariners in the business, she would never have survived. But she did, after twenty-four hours of incredibly difficult navigation, she saw Cape Spartel astern. To compensate for what she had undergone, she then proceeded to sink 25,000 tons of enemy shipping during a thirty-days' cruise. When she returned it was to Bordeaux where the Italian Atlantic Base had by then been set up.

I shall have more to say later of Bordeaux and the Atlantic

Base. It is an interesting subject which so far has been ignored in accounts of the war. But now we must come back to *Malaspina*. Of the 25,000 tons of shipping which she sent to the bottom, 12,000 were represented by the tanker *British Fame*. Leoni has already told the story in his entertaining memoirs; but at least the outline must be given here, partly because the sinking of *British Fame* was our first major success in the Atlantic and partly because it gave rise to an episode which does honor to Italian seamen.

The tanker was sighted one morning at half-light before dawn. *Malaspina* was on the surface, the officer of the watch and lookouts were on the bridge and the captain was dozing in a deckchair below, when something loomed up close by. Alarm! Crash dive. When Leoni examined the target through the periscope he saw that what the lookout had spotted was a large tanker, armed with two medium guns and zigzagging at high speed. A splendid target for a submarine. He closed in for the kill, fired his first salvo of two torpedoes at 15,000 yards and then dove to await results. Just before firing he had seen that the tanker was flying British colors. Now he waited, watch in hand, counting the seconds. He calculated that it would take the torpedoes ninety seconds to reach their mark and, sure enough, at ninety-four seconds exactly, *Malaspina* felt a dull concussion through her hull, followed by a second slighter one. Apparently a hit. Leoni raised his periscope for another look. There was the intrepid tanker, still steady on her course, sailing along as if nothing had happened It looked like a miss after all. This was at once confirmed by a hail of shot round the periscope. In such cases there is only one thing to do—dive as quickly as possible and get out of the way, so as to evade the gunfire, the search and the final bomb or depth charge. Later, with luck, one may be able to try again.

Malaspina went down to about 160 feet. Presently, the hydrophone operator reported that he could hear nothing. Not a propeller was turning in the neighborhood. The tanker must have stopped and if so. . . . Up went the periscope again and there she was, still floating, still on an even keel, but this time undoubtedly stationary. The torpedoes had evidently reached their mark—the initial detonation showed that—but their effect must have been muffled for the first few minutes, perhaps by flooding. Enough damage had been done to stop the ship, but not to sink her.

Leoni fired a third torpedo. It struck directly beneath the funnel and sent up a column of water which could be clearly seen through the periscope. But the tanker still stayed there, apparently undamaged. With three torpedoes inside her, she refused to sink or catch fire and did not even appear to be crippled. Obviously a phenomenon. *Malaspina*, still submerged, closed her sufficiently to read the name on her stern: *British Fame*. Leoni called his officers to the periscope in turn to see this extraordinary sight of a tanker motionless in the middle of the sea, with her guns manned and her flag flying. Then at last it was seen that she was lowering a boat on her port side.

It took another two hours and two more torpedoes to sink *British Fame*. When it was over, Leoni was left with the problem of what to do with the ship's crew, which had been saved almost to a man. All Italian submariners, especially in those early months of the war, found the idea of turning a crew adrift extremely repugnant. Once they had taken to the boats they were no longer enemies but fellow human beings and, what is more, fellow seamen. The instinct to save life at sea, when it can be saved, is strong in all sailors; an ingrained part of their nature. And no one—no sailor of whatever nationality—can instantaneously strip himself of all his humanity, even in war time, and least of all in this part of it. For these reasons, Leoni did not find his problem an easy one.

Later in the war, our submarine commanders received categorical orders to do nothing whatever for the crews of ships that they sank. But in August 1940 these orders had not yet been issued. Accordingly—and there is nothing surprising in this—Leoni took *British Fame's* boats in tow. It meant proceeding on the surface for a day and a night. He did not drop the tow until they had reached a position off the Azores where it was certain that the British crew would be safe.

Since we are on this subject, I may as well add that orders to disregard the safety of survivors were only issued after the setting up of the Atlantic Base. Before that, much was left to the initiative of individual captains who were generally able to find a way out of their difficulties. But after the establishment of the Bordeaux base, our part in commerce-raiding—in "unrestricted warfare" if you like—had to be fitted into the framework of what our German allies were doing. It was then that our commanders received their sad education in the exigencies of war.

However, no new orders, not even those of the German U-boat command, were wholly able to eradicate the natural humanity of Italian seamen. They always managed to give what help they could to crews who had abandoned ship. It was, of course, out of the question to take them on board. But they gave them food, water and medical stores; or towed their boats for a few hours till they were nearer land; or even, as Leoni did with the crew of *British Fame* or Todaro, whom we shall come to presently, with the crew of the *Cabalho*, took them in tow for twenty-four hours. And even so, no Italian submarine came back from an operation without some story of what it had cost her crew to carry out orders and abandon survivors to the mercy of the sea, to cold and perhaps hunger and thirst.

II

Betasom

So far I have given some account of our submarines passing through the Strait of Gibraltar to operate against British shipping in the Atlantic and have just mentioned the new base which was afterwards set up on the right bank of the Gironde. But I may not have made it clear that these Atlantic operations were not simply an idea of some higher-up in the Admiralty, but were the result of careful study by the Naval Staff before the war. We had always intended to operate against British shipping, if war came; and in 1940 we did so by the only means available. It meant working from our home bases and risking the double passage of the Straits under the conditions which I have described. But there was no other way out. It was either that or give up the whole idea—a thing we were unwilling to do, not so much for reasons of prestige, as because there was no operational alternative. We had no choice but to rely on the skill of our commanders and to expose them to great hazards at both ends of each trip.

As soon as the Germans had occupied France and were in control of the coastline as far south as the Bay of Biscay, the situation changed. Our Naval Staff began at once to investigate the possibility of setting up a permanent base at one of the French Atlantic ports and operating part of our large submarine fleet from there. The question was submitted to the German Admiralty and the Army of Occupation, both of whom gave their cordial assent. As a result, in August 1940, an Italian base began to take shape at Bordeaux.

To begin with it was simply called the Atlantic Flotilla; but this was evidently too prosaic for the brass hats in Rome, who presently re-christened it "High Command of Italian Submarine Forces in the Atlantic." This sonorous title was rather long for everyday use, so it was cut down in practice to *Betasom*. You can derive that how you please—*Beta* for *B*ordeaux or *B*ase and *Som* for *Som*mergibili. Anyway, that was what the base was normally called and the title has stuck ever since.

The command of *Betasom* was assigned to Rear Admiral Angelo Parona. In the first war, he had served in submarines in the Adriatic. Between the wars, as soon as our submarine strength began to grow again, he had commanded a flotilla; and, immediately before his appointment to *Betasom*, he had been the Number Two in Submarine Command. He was a man of parts and one, above all, who knew how to get things done. No one could have been quicker or more resourceful in finding a way through the many difficulties that beset him. But he was not, perhaps, an entirely sympathetic character. He expected everyone to put as much into the job as he did himself; and he made no effort to hide his feelings, if any of his subordinates fell below his own high standard. As a result he was apt to be impatient and the impatience was sometimes resented. On the other hand, he never stinted praise; he could be relied on to take official notice of acts of courage, and he was always willing to encourage enthusiasts and those whom he recognized as fighters. It was due to Parona's skill and drive that *Betasom* so quickly reached the state of efficiency which enabled it not only to refit submarines on their return from operations, but also to carry out the major repairs made necessary by bad weather or enemy action. He was also able to do much to improve the design and equipment of submarines for their specialized work in the Atlantic.

Spezia was the depot from which men and materials were drafted for *Betasom*. The same base also provided the largest contingent of Atlantic submarines. Spezia also contributed its commanding officer, Commander Aldo Cocchia, who was appointed chief of staff of *Betasom*. On him fell the responsibility for collecting and transporting to Bordeaux everything that the new base was likely to need. "Everything" ran from dynamos for battery charging to special rations; from engine spares to optical instruments; from cigarettes to a complete radio station; from clothing to air compressors; from small arms and guns to ammunition; from torpedoes to machine tools for the workshop. From Spezia, too, came the roster of officers, seamen and shipwrights, all of whom had to be provided with transportation, rations and travel orders. Finally, in August 1940, from Spezia, came Admiral Parona and part of his staff.

In Bordeaux the Admiral found himself confronted by a row of empty, dirty sheds, which had previously been used as warehouses. There were no dockyard facilities and not so much as the smell of a workshop. No electric light or power was connected. He held his first conference that evening in one of the deserted sheds. All his staff attended, sitting around on packing cases. There was Major Fenu, who later ran *Betasom's* small but highly efficient dockyard; Lieutenant Commander De Moratti, the signal officer; Commander Capone, in charge of supplies; Lieutenant Colonel Di Losa, the administration officer; Lieutenant Commander Giudice, the Admiral's secretary and flag lieutenant; and Major Crucilla, the medical officer. Only two officers were missing; Lieutenant Auconi, the gunnery officer, who joined later but made up for lost time; and the chief of staff, who was due to arrive in October in command of the submarine *Torelli*.

The plan of the future base was drawn in chalk on the floor. Storerooms here; engine shop there; spares in that shed; generator over there; compressors arranged this way; electric wiring like that; transmitter in the other place. All orders were brisk and oral: "You take this over; you take that over." Then everyone set to work, urged on by the Admiral, who gave instructions, settled problems, bulldozed his way through difficulties. It all had to be done under the critical eyes of the Germans and the implied mockery of the French, who seemed to be saying: "Well, let's see how these Italians make out." But the work went on with enthusiasm, with self-confidence and verve which produces results.

The harbor's wetdocks, separated from the river by two locks, had been turned over to us. There, alongside the quays at which the submarines would later berth, rose the workshops, the stores, the electric plant, the compressors, the armory and the torpedo stores—all the components of a large submarine base. The Germans had also handed over the French transatlantic liner *De Grasse*, which was berthed along the outer quay of the dock. We found her very useful during the first few weeks and quartered ourselves on board, along with the operations room and the administration offices, our wardroom, the sickbay and the main radio station. She managed to accommodate everyone, from the Admiral to the submarine crews, from the dockyard hands to the stewards and waiters supplied by Lloyd Triestino. As time went on and our numbers increased, we had to requisition another liner, the *Usaramo*, which lay astern of the *De Grasse*. She provided sleeping quarters and messrooms for the many workmen who had in the meantime arrived from Italy. Even so, materials and spares tended to overflow into various sheds on the quay.

At last everything was organized as it should be. And then, on 8 December 1940, our burgeoning base suffered a heavy air raid. It lasted five hours. The *Usaramo* was sunk; a small steamer nearby was hit and went up in flames; bombs fell on the sheds, on the stores, on the dockside and on our motor transport which was parked there. We were obliged to recognize that our beautiful organization had one weakness. True, the submarines, the main target, were miraculously undamaged and the *De Grasse* had only received some ghastly but harmless hits on her upper works. But there was no reason to expect that we would be so lucky again. We had made the mistake of concentrating too much into far too small a space. It was now clear that we would have to disperse. The first step was to find other quarters for the submarine crews, who had every right to peace and quiet between operations. For the rest, we would have to give up the convenience of having everything close at hand. The submarines would have to be left as they were, since there was no other berth. But the office staff, most of the stores, the workshops, the armory and the ammunition dumps would have to find another location. And with them—at least at night, which seemed to be the time for air raids—would have to go all personnel not strictly necessary for guard duties.

The problem seemed far from easy; but in fact it was quickly solved, thanks to the Admiral's organizing ability and—I must add—the energetic and efficient help of our German allies. A few telephone calls, an exchange of messages between *Betasom* and U-boat Command, and a new organization sprang to life. The crews and stores were accommodated in sheds outside the danger zone; officers were billeted in villas or, if they were lucky, in neighboring *chateaux;* and headquarters, with its offices, mess and radio station, set up in a small house not far from the submarine berth. The re-organization was complete by January 1941, and remained in being until the Armistice.

III

U-Boats

THE Italian submarines at Bordeaux, and *Betasom* itself, came under the operational control of the German U-boat Command. But for administration and discipline we were still responsible to the Italian Submarine High-Command, *Maricosom*, in Rome. We were thus in two distinct chains of command; but the fact never hampered us or gave rise to any difficulty. Rome was always careful not to give operational orders and the *B.d.U* (U-boat Command) never interfered administratively. What was important to the German Command was to have the effective control of our twenty-seven submarines. For the rest they were willing to rely on the spirit of co-operation which then united our two countries' forces. And in this they were right. No one at *Betasom* had thoughts for anything but victory. We were all convinced that victory could only be won by working as closely as possible with the Germans.

We thus became part of the German organization and were most cordially welcomed. Naturally so, when you consider that the Italian Atlantic Flotilla exactly doubled the number of submarines available to the *Kriegsmarine* for the war against British shipping. That may seem surprising, for estimates of the size of the German submarine fleet were often rather vague and indefinite. It may be as well, therefore, to begin by stating the facts. At the outbreak of war Germany had no more than forty U-boats, of which only half were operational. The German High

Command, especially on its naval side, had certainly foreseen the importance of the war on shipping; and yet submarines—the one indispensable instrument—were lacking. Was this due to a failure on the part of the Naval Staff or to a political misjudgment of the European situation? There is no certain answer; but the fact remains that in September 1939 Germany had only a few dozen submarines, mostly small and not very seaworthy. Of these she could only send out six or seven on patrol at a time and often less.

One story, current at the time, shows the situation clearly. At the end of December 1939, only three U-boats were operating in the whole Atlantic. By an odd chance they were commanded by three brothers, all naval lieutenants—the brothers Sachs. German submariners used to say, justifiably enough, that the blockade of the British Isles had become a private war on the part of the Sachs family.

Nevertheless, the German Navy had trained its submarine crews well. They had carried out exercises in attacking convoys, organized and escorted as it had been estimated the British would. These exercises, each lasting several days, evolved the wolfpack tactics which Admiral Doenitz later used with so much success against British and American shipping.

The commentators have since had much to say about these tactics; but they have, I think, missed or underestimated one point of the greatest importance—the liberty of action which was allowed to individual commanders. Doenitz relied, not on issuing detailed orders, but on grounding his officers in certain basic principles which were to guide their actions. He believed, quite rightly, that if the submarine commanders were properly indoctrinated, there would be no need for elaborate restrictions and directives. Each commander would know what he ought to do in any given situation and would be able to rely on his own skill and knowledge to find the answer to the hundred-and-one problems which present themselves in action.

Even patrol areas were not rigidly defined. Each submarine

in the Atlantic was allotted an area of operations, so to speak; but this was only her starting point. Any commander—novices included—was free to shift his position, as often and as far as he liked, in search of enemy convoys. The star performers—Prien, Kretschmer, Lüth and others—were given unrestricted orders, which allowed them to indulge in what came to be known as a "free-hunt" without any restrictions as to time or place.

The U-boats operated on the surface. Once at sea, each commander acted independently and made his own search, casting in this direction or that according to the clues he could pick up for himself or which were provided by an occasional signal. Sometimes he followed his own instinct entirely, more often the advice and suggestions of *B.d.U.* Days or even weeks might pass without result. Then, at last, one of the U-boats would sight the enemy, a close-packed convoy of thirty or forty ships—part of England's lifeline—with its antisubmarine escort, perhaps a shadowing aircraft and sometimes a supporting force of aircraft carriers and cruisers. As soon as a convoy was sighted, all the U-boats in the vicinity—if possible all those at sea—converged on its track. But it was essential that the original U-boat should not attack at once, lest the convoy disperse. Her task was to report the position of the convoy and keep track of its subsequent movements. The technique of shadowing was to lie back on the horizon during the day and close up at night, signalling changes of course at regular intervals. It meant sticking to the convoy like a limpet, running either awash or openly on the surface, playing catch-as-catch-can with aircraft and escort vessels. To keep up with a fast convoy the diesels had to be run at full speed, so that the low-lying submarine took on green seas right over the bridge. But the lookouts, lashed to the rail with safety-belts never lost sight of the ships they were following. Their position, course and speed was regularly reported. Sometimes, at the request of *B.d.U,* the shadowing U-boat would transmit homing signals to the other submarines in the area.

This repeated signalling ended inevitably in revealing the

U-boat's presence. The enemy would then take every possible evasive action, laying down smoke and making sudden changes of course, and would counterattack with destroyers, corvettes and aircraft. Each gambit produced its reply, each move by the convoy a countermove by the U-boat, so that the two duellists were locked in a tense struggle, marked by sudden turns, rapid dives, gunfire, torpedoes and patterns of depth-charges.

Meanwhile, as soon as the first sighting report had been received, the *B.d.U* had called up all the other submarines at sea. The position of each was known at headquarters and it was decided there which boat could—and therefore should—join the fight, even if it meant a forty-eight hours' chase. It was also decided which U-boat was the nearest to the scene of action and could join the shadower at once, help her to keep track of the convoy and replace her, if she became a casualty.

The order to start the attack proper always came direct from headquarters and was given as soon as Doenitz was satisfied that enough U-boats were in touch with the convoy to destroy it. The attack was made on the surface at night. As soon as darkness fell, the wolves ran in among the flock—the convoy which could neither shake them off nor destroy them—and the battle began. One blow followed another, delivered at a range at which it was impossible to miss, between opponents who could barely see each other. The U-boats, still on the surface, came down the lanes between the ships, each picking her own target and staying abreast till it had been destroyed by torpedoes or gunfire. Ships sank, ships took fire. All of them fought, for they were all armed, and the escorts fought the hardest. They threw themselves on the submarines wherever they could find them, hit some and forced others to dive. But once the wolves were among the sheep, the dogs could do little to bring them to bay.[1] The convoy dispersed and the faster ships tried to make a getaway. But the

---

[1] I am speaking, of course, of the period 1940-41; later the allies developed a defense which was largely effective against U-boat attack.

U-boats still clung on, following and keeping up the attack. The escorts were generally left alone, unless there was an exceptionally favorable opportunity, for the submarines' real business was to destroy the convoy, to wipe out merchant tonnage. These encounters lasted the whole night and into the following day, or even for two or three days, if necessary. All the time fresh U-boats were joining in, brought to the scene by radio messages from sinking ships or by signals from the original pack reporting their successes.

And so the running fight went on. . . .

IV

Shift to the Atlantic

AT the end of 1939 only a handful of U-boats were ready for Atlantic operations. By the summer of 1940 there were not many more, for the building program was still in its early stages and may not even have been finally settled. The Italian reinforcement was therefore very welcome. It gave a new impetus to the campaign against British shipping, which then seemed the only means, short of an invasion of England, by which the war could finally be won. Accordingly, our main submarine fleet was transferred to *Betasom* to operate side by side with the German U-boats.

Malaspina, after her first Atlantic patrol, had already homed on *Betasom* instead of returning to Italy. She was presently followed by twenty-six other boats—four from Taranto, eight from Naples and fifteen from Spezia. These included three—*Calvi*, *Finzi* and *Veniero*—which had each completed one Atlantic mission in June and July and returned to base in Italy. To the six transits through the Straits already mentioned, we must therefore add another twenty-seven, making thirty-three in all. We shall come to others later. During August and September our submarines went through at the rate of one a night. Some made the passage submerged, some on the surface. Some got through without incident and even without noticing the adverse current at Gibraltar or the eddies off Tarifa. Others were less fortunate and became involved in tricky feats of navigation or

Shift to the Atlantic 19

a battle of wits with enemy destroyers. But they all reached the Atlantic—including *Calvi,* who had much the same difficulty as *Malaspina,* and *Bianchi* and *Brin,* who ran into trouble one after the other.

Bianchi (Lt. Cdr. Giovannini) had already completed one tour of duty in the approaches to the Straits, where she had torpedoed and sunk an enemy patrol ship. Now she returned to the same waters with a certain amount of experience. She took the passage submerged, but went off course either because she was being hunted or because she was caught in the Tarifa current, and ended by hitting the bottom somewhere off Point Malabata. She reported serious damage to the pressure hull, which prevented her from diving again, but was able to make Tangier on the surface. This was an international port and therefore free to all nations.

Brin (Lt. Longanesi) had a similar misfortune, or one with the same results. While submerged she damaged both her gyro and her magnetic compass. Longanesi tried to use a small, uncompensated boat's compass, but the navigation was too tricky for such rough and ready methods. The end came when *Brin* ran ashore off Malabata Point and damaged her hull. Longanesi, unable either to continue his patrol or to return to base, also made for Tangier, where two Italian submarines found themselves uninvited guests.

The British, of course stationed destroyers on guard outside the harbor and set their local agents to work. Our people, on the other hand, carried out repairs with spare parts sent from Italy and, after three weeks' work, were ready for what proved a brilliant and successful maneuver.

It was a calm, clear, moonlit night. The two commanders were at the club. The crews were dozing in their bunks; and on the quayside Spanish guards were sleepily keeping watch. Everything seemed quiet and still. Suddenly, at a prearranged time, the two commanders reappeared on board; the crews sprang to action stations as if by magic; *Bianchi* and *Brin* slipped their cables and were off. Traveling on the surface, both diesels wide open, they ran the gauntlet of waiting destroyers and got clear beyond Cape Spartel, leaving behind them baffled British agents.

Off the mouth of the Gironde, *Brin* found a British submarine lying in wait and was greeted by gunfire almost at her own doorstep. She returned the greeting cordially. A heavy fog was then lying on the sea, which gave this little brush a fantastic, unreal quality. The result was love all, or perhaps one should say, advantage to Longanesi, since he succeeded in entering the Gironde. The English had only the satisfaction of a little gunplay.

Among the submarines to reach Bordeaux in the summer of 1940 was *Torelli*. The following extract from her captain's log gives a clear picture of what the passage through the Straits was like:

"We dived at dawn on 7 September within sight of Alboran Island and, so as to make certain of our point of departure, remained on the bottom all day. At nightfall we surfaced and set a course for the lighthouse on Carnero Point, running on the surface under one diesel. Speed, about 10 knots; no moon; sea calm; light westerly breezes. At 0200 hours on 8 September we dived, being then two miles south of the Rock. No ships were sighted while we were on the surface; and there was no hydrophone effect when we reached our planned depth of 290 ft., which we expected to hold for the whole passage.

"Making allowances for adverse currents, we had estimated about 18 hours for the passage. In fact, it took nearly 22; but on the whole there was little trouble. No enemy ship was sighted. Once or twice the hydrophones picked up the beat of a nearby propeller. On one occasion it seemed as if we were being hunted, for we could hear the noise of an engine stopping and starting, always very close. The buzz went round and there were a few signs of nervousness among the crew. But no depth-charges followed, nor did we pick up the characteristic high note of the enemy's Asdic. It was probably a Spanish fishing boat, intent on her own business.

"Navigation, on the otherhand, especially in the strong contrary currents, gave us some trouble, though nothing serious. We were able to keep steerage way at about four knots and hold our depth within 30 ft. We experienced none of those violent surges of 120 or 150 ft., of which *Calvi, Malaspina* and others had complained. It had been suggested that we should cut out the auxiliary motors, partly to economize battery power, but mainly to reduce detectable noise. But, finding the boat difficult to handle with unassisted steering, we ended by keeping everything going. And in any case, anyone hunting a submerged submarine would be more likely to use apparatus of the Asdic type, which cannot be thrown off by silencing machinery.

"Shortly after our first dive the echo-sounder showed a progressively diminishing reading, although in that part of the Straits the soundings should have been constant. Evidently we had lost the main channel; but it was difficult to know whether the strong lateral current, reported by almost all submarines, was carrying us north or south. Although considerable drift was apparent after ten minutes or so, it was another half-hour before the soundings confirmed that the set was southerly. We were obliged to change course, making allowance for the estimated strength of the current. Apart from some disturbed motion and sudden variations of trim, nothing abnormal further happened until about noon. Then our difficulties began, when by dead reckoning Tarifa was abeam. This was an area where everyone ran into trouble. In our case, we found that we were barely making headway.

"This was a point at which the seabed should have shelved steeply upwards. Instead, soundings remained constant or even increased. Steering and trimming were both very difficult and there were moments when we seemed about to lose control altogether. This was the crisis—a crisis which lasted for four hours.

"We were all in the control room. The skipper was on his stool with his eyes going from the depth gauge to the chart; the executive officer was squatting beside him. The chief was at the *fruit-machine*,[1] which plotted the soundings read off by the petty officer. The helmsman watched compass and rudder and gave warning when we were off course, as happened fairly often. It was pretty cold and we were all wearing heavy sweaters. The executive officer had thrown a blanket over his shoulders as well, so that we looked like a group of gypsies around a campfire.

"To save battery power, lighting had been reduced to a minimum. There was one dim bulb over the depth gauge and another in the middle of the control room. In that dim light everyone looked gaunt and hollow-eyed and the general effect was that of a surrealist picture. Condensation dripped from the plating of the hull. The watertight doors were closed. The rest of the crew were ostensibly resting on their bunks; but certainly no one slept. They were all intent on what was happening, ready to leap to their feet as soon as an emergency arose, for which all hands would be needed.

"The deep silence was only broken by the petty officer reading off the soundings, by the helmsman's low voice or by occasional orders from the skipper. Periodically the electrician's mate would appear with specific gravity readings from the batteries and, after conferring with the chief, would report how we stood in battery power.

"It soon became clear that, by keeping a course through the middle of the Straits, we were making far too little progress. We therefore decided to bear up under the Moroccan coast,

---

[1] The air-valve group; its Italian nickname *pianoforte*.

partly in the hope of picking up a favorable current and partly because the more even distribution of soundings suggested that navigation would be easier. We altered course 30 degrees to the south and then turned west again as soon as the soundings showed that we had 150 ft. of water beneath us.

"The critical phase lasted, as I said, for about four hours. After that there was a marked improvement. As soon as we came in under the coast, we found a favorable current which carried us out through the Straits. It became easier to hold our course and, in short, from then on everything ran smoothly.

"At 1800 hours we freshened the air, more for the sake of testing the apparatus than from any real need. Two hours later we had a meal. Finally, at 2300 hours, reckoning that we were now far enough out, we made a careful check all round with the hydrophones and surfaced. We came up with the diesels already clutched in and a salvo of torpedoes ready to fire, if any destroyers were in sight. I was the first on the bridge. We had surfaced near a cluster of fishing boats' lights, with Cape Spartel bearing seven or eight miles to the east. Over the inter-com I told the crew that we had passed the Straits. An answering voice came from below: '*Viva l'Italia!*'"

As we have seen a total of twenty-seven submarines got through into the Atlantic. Each of them remained about a month on patrol, operating against shipping in the area of the Azores. This was a good station, partly because weather conditions were generally favorable and partly because most of the enemy merchant ships in that part of the Atlantic, though armed, were sailing independently. It was an excellent training ground for submarine crews with no previous experience in the tactics of commerce raiding. I don't know, for example, whether any Italian submarine commander had carried out a peacetime exercise in attacking convoys by night on the surface—the accepted tactic during the war. I don't know; but I doubt it. Nor do I believe that more than three or four commanders had ever taken a submarine into the Atlantic. It was helpful, therefore, that they should gain a little experience in a quiet area before facing bad weather and the British in the western Atlantic.

It was for these reasons that we picked on the Azores; and this area became the scene of our first successes in a campaign which turned out, on the whole, not too badly. During their activities, the thirty-two Italian submarines operating exclusively in the Atlantic sank about one million tons of enemy shipping. On her first patrol *Malaspina* sank the *British Fame* and two other ships; *Cappellini* sank the *Cabalho*, of which more later; Polizzi's *Nani* sank two ships and Petroni's *Veniero* and Bertarelli's *Baracca* one each. To these should probably be added others which I do not remember. *Mocenigo* (Lt. Cdr. Agostini) hooked an entire convoy, played it with great skill, reported its position and herself sank two ships.

These results could be called fairly satisfactory—especially, if you consider the crews' lack of training and the fact that our submarines were neither well designed nor well equipped for the work they had to do. The first requirement which was lacking was a high surface speed, in order to shadow effectively. The second was a low silhouette to make the submarine difficult to spot on the surface. Unfortunately, Italian submarines were equipped with conning towers of truly prodigious size, which provided space for galleys, lavatories and what have you. It would also have been a help if there had been altogether less superstructure, whereas the bridge was in fact dominated by the two massive periscope housings to which were attached the radio aerials and a short mast.

If you ask the reason for this unrealistic design, I can only say that few people in Italy expected before the war that our submarines would do most of their fighting on the surface—at any rate in the early days and in the Atlantic—and would only submerge occasionally. Hence the unnecessary superstructure, the low surface-speed and the unsatisfactory hull design.

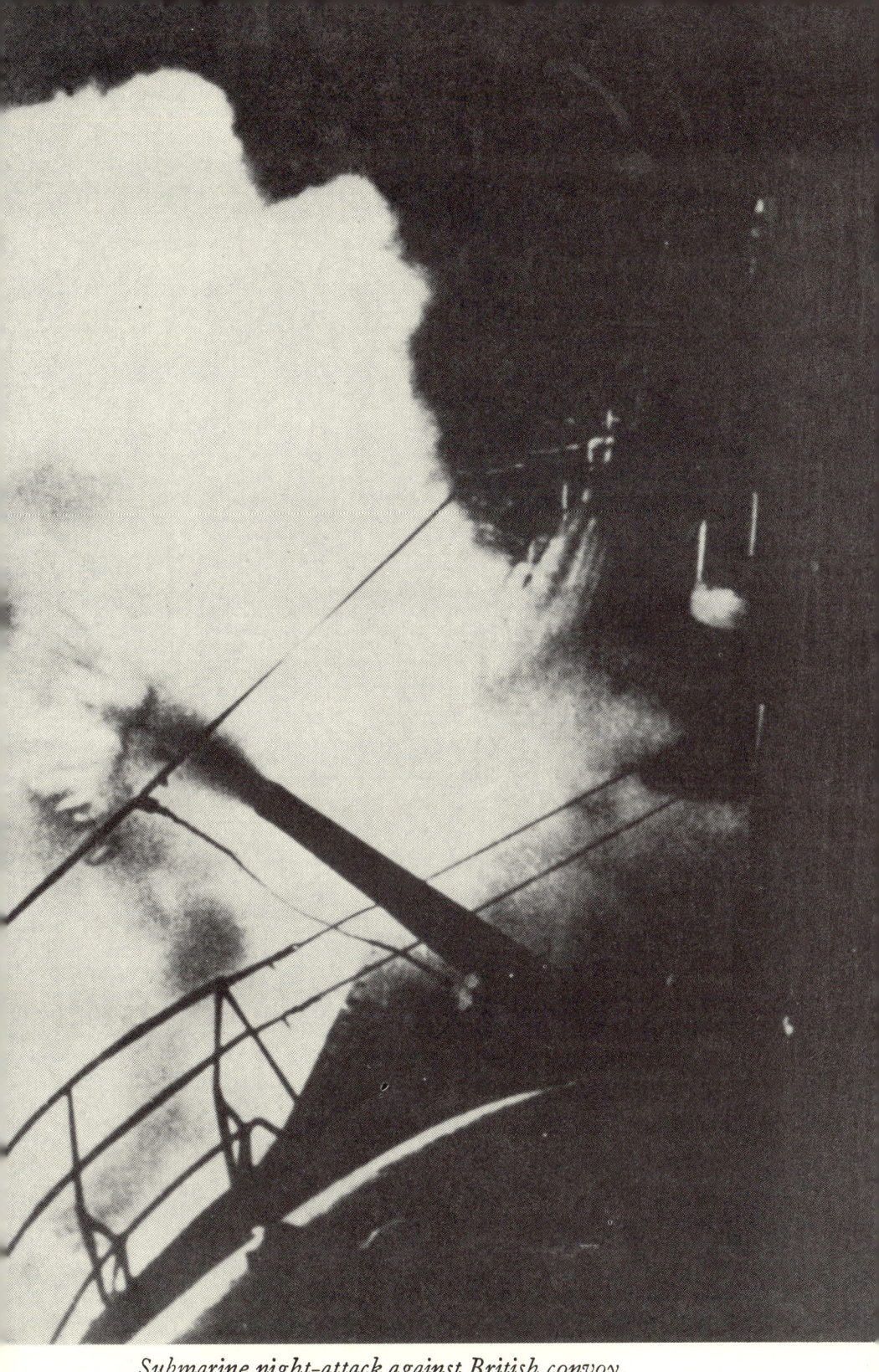

Submarine night-attack against British convoy.

Italian submarine cruising in the North Atlantic

Italian submarine entering Bordeaux do[ck]

Shift to the Atlantic 25

These faults soon came to light at *Betasom*. Alterations were effected with that base's usual promptness. Under the direction of Fenu, our engineer, radical changes in hull design were made and pushed through at record speed, despite our limited resources, the shortage of skilled hands and the interruption of air raids and air raid warnings. In this work the staff at *Betasom* had, of course, the full collaboration of the various submarine commanders; and we were in fact largely guided by their reports, observations and requests.

It fell to one of the first submarines remodelled at *Betasom* to achieve one of our most striking successes in the Atlantic. Giovannini's *Bianchi*—the same *Bianchi* that had so much trouble in the Straits—was completely refitted and re-designed at Bordeaux. She then set out for her station, where she received a signal ordering her to attack a convoy which a German U-boat was then shadowing. Closing at full speed, Giovannini found the convoy early on the second night, when the German wolf-pack attack had already begun. He squeezed himself into the battle, sank two ships straight away and gave chase to a third. When he got within range and was about to fire his torpedoes, he found that a U-boat was also closing in for the kill. A kind of race then started between the two submarines, different from a race in a regatta only in that the prize was the sinking of a ship. It was an incident which German propaganda made much of later, all the more so because Giovannini was a well-known figure at pre-war Kiel regattas, where he had often won first place for the Navy.

The end of the story was that both submarines fired at once and both hit. The unfortunate ship sank immediately, followed by another which *Bianchi* caught in the same chase. As soon as the destruction of the convoy was complete, Giovannini headed happily homewards, most of his torpedoes fired and his fuel almost exhausted. On the way back he had another success, his fifth victim, and arrived at Bordeaux with 30,000 tons of enemy shipping to his credit. For a long time, until Fecia De Cossato appeared on the scene, this stood as a record for a single patrol.

After this success Giovannini was transferred to Gotenhafen, where he established a school for Italian submariners, and *Bianchi* was taken over by Franco Tosoni Pittoni, of whom we shall have more to say later.

V

Salvatore Todaro, the Knight Errant

I FIRST met Salvatore Todaro when he brought *Cappellini* into Bordeaux and, in the Admiral's absence, made his report to me on his first and notable Atlantic patrol. Though I had never seen him before our brief interview was enough to convince me of his qualities. Later, as I came to know him better, my admiration for him developed into a deep affection. He was a good deal my junior both in years and service; but he was naturally mature and had a strength and nobility of character which would have made anyone proud to claim his friendship.

He was a stockily built man of medium height, olive-skinned, with a pair of keen, thoughtful black eyes, which exactly matched his short curly beard. Before the war he had been, among other things, an observer on flying duties and had suffered internal injuries in a crash, which, though there were no outward signs, caused him considerable pain. This forced him to go slow for a while; but in June 1940, when it was clear that Italy would come into the war, he volunteered at once for active service. In fact, he made repeated applications for a submarine command in the Atlantic—about the most exhausting job that you can imagine. The Admiralty, knowing something about his physical condition, put him off for several weeks; but in the end the exigencies of war and the shortage of submarine commanders prevailed, and Todaro was ordered to *Cappellini*, whose original commander, Masi, had just left for the newly established school at Pola.

Cappellini's gun-battle with a British destroyer in the Straits has already been described. In the autumn of 1940 she made the passage again under Todaro's command. There is no point in going into details, which would only be repetitive. It is enough to say that Todaro, like others, reached the Atlantic after twenty-four hours of adventurous navigation below the surface. Then began the usual long, weary patrol in bad weather, the unremitting search for a target, which had to be carried out on the surface, no matter what the conditions, lest any chance of sighting an enemy should be missed. At last, after a fortnight at sea, a distant silhouette was picked up one morning at dawn. Todaro attacked. His target, as he discovered later, was the Portuguese ship *Cabalho*, then under charter to the British, with a cargo of crated aircraft. He attacked boldly on the surface, as he always did, using his guns rather than torpedoes. This method of attack was typical of Todaro and earned a caustic comment from Doenitz in the margin of one of his reports: "It is a pity that this officer is not commanding a gunboat." It was not kindly meant; but it was a tribute, all the same, to a certain quixotic vein in Todaro's character.

The *Cabalho* sank quickly after a short fight which became commonplace during the war. There would be no need to say any more, if it were not for Todaro's subsequent actions. The story is worth telling, if only in outline, because it made quite a stir at the time, both in Italy and abroad. What happened, in short, was that Todaro, like Leoni before him, was faced with the quandary of what to do with the crew of the ship he had sunk. Should they be left to take their chance in the ship's boat or taken on board *Cappellini* during the weeks when she would still be at sea? Todaro's whole character was against the first solution and the second was physically impossible. So he adopted a third, which was to take the boat in tow for nearly 600 miles across the Atlantic. It meant exposing himself and his command to a serious risk by sailing at reduced speed on the surface, an easy prey to enemy destroyers and aircraft. But he did it and duly brought *Cabalho's* crew to safety, dropping the tow when they were within sight of land.

This episode brought Todaro a severe reprimand when he got back to Bordeaux. From the operational point of view it was richly deserved. But one would not be sorry to see more people earn reprimands of this kind, in peace as well as in war; it would strengthen one's confidence in the human race. Even at the time, Todaro had supporters as well as critics. People he had never heard of—including some from enemy countries—wrote to him in gratitude and admiration. I saw one of these letters: It was from a Portuguese woman who saluted him as an "angel of goodness" and *"chevalier sans peur et sans reproche."* It was not a bad description.

A couple of months later, after a rest and a thorough re-fit, *Cappellini* left again for the Atlantic, this time for a particularly difficult mission off West Africa. I remember seeing her when she sailed. She looked like a racing-car, stripped for an event, with all superfluities removed. She had taken on extra fuel and was lying very low in the water with her deck almost awash. Her two four-inch guns were shining and her conning tower was stripped of all its hamper. Her crew, lined up on deck in their greys, looked proud of their boat and her captain. Each of them had a dirk in his belt. Looking at these, someone suggested that Todaro's plan was to capture enemy ships by boarding, like a buccaneer. But those who knew him better saw the point. The dirks were not a boy's thriller version of modern war, but an emblem designed to raise the morale of the crew on a difficult operation. The only man who carried no arms at all was Todaro himself. So far as I know, he never did—an appropriate gesture from a man of his character and make-up.

Cappellini left for her billet three thousand miles to the south, in an area where, up to December 1940, no German or Italian submarine had operated. It was a virgin field, but one of vital importance to British trade, where surprise would be the essence of the attack. The first few days of the patrol were without incident. Winter in the Bay of Biscay was replaced by spring off Rio di Oro and then by summer off Senegal. The first brush with the enemy occurred off Cape Verde and was a surface action with the armed merchantman *Aeumeus*, of seven thousand tons. *Cappellini* soon beat down her defense and sank her. Her next encounter about in the latitude of Freetown, was with another armed merchantman, the eight-thousand-ton *Shakespeare*, then acting as a troopship. She had three four-inch guns and a number of machine guns and was evidently under the command of a gallant and energetic captain.

The action began about eight in the morning and was fought in Todaro's characteristic style on the surface. This time *Cappellini* had a tough and dogged opponent; and the duel, which lasted about four hours, was hardfought on both sides. When Todaro opened fire, the *Shakespeare* hit back with her four-inch guns and tried to escape. *Cappellini* gave chase and, having a higher surface speed, was able to close to point-blank range. The Englishman redoubled his defense. *Cappellini* was swept by shell and machine gun fire and her guncrews suffered heavy casualties. Engineers and engineroom ratings, released from duty below, clamored for permission to join in the fight. Among them was Lieut. (E) Stiepovich. He saw the machine-gunner fall and asked for "the honor of taking his post." The phrase might have come out of a storybook, but I have quoted it exactly. Permission was given and he took the gunner's place, only to be seriously wounded himself by a shell splinter. He refused to ge carried below because, as he said, he wanted to be in at the death.

At last, about noon, the *Shakespeare,* riddled by gunfire and hit by at least one torpedo, caught fire and sank. Meanwhile, in reply to an SOS, a British aircraft from Freetown had appeared on the scene. Todaro made an emergency dive; but the first aircraft was soon followed by others and then by corvettes and other antisubmarine craft. A furious hunt was on, it lasted all that day, all night and all the day following.

Below in the submarine, where he had been carried when they dived, Stiepovich was in agony, but made no complaint. All he asked was to see the ship's flag before he died; and Todaro left the control room for a few minutes to spread it out before him. This again sounds like a scene from a book—a book written in the days before chauvinism had taken a grip on the world. But it was in fact a scene from real life between two men to whom the words "country" and "flag" had a more than rhetorical meaning. Its setting was a submerged submarine, shaken by depth charges and already in serious danger from damage sustained in early fighting.

Thanks to the skill and steady nerves of her captain and crew, *Cappellini* made good her escape. But when she finally reached Bordeaux, she was little better than a wreck. Four months' work was needed to put her into shape again.

After completing three patrols in the Atlantic and sinking some 25,000 tons of enemy shipping, Todaro took a holiday. That is to say, he transferred to the naval Commandos and was given the job of raising and training a flotilla of midget submarines, which were intended for operations in the Black Sea. I caught a glimpse of his patient, meticulous work when I was at Spezia, fitting out the *Da Recco* as a convoy escort. Todaro was there too with his one-man submarines of the B and C Types and we used to meet to discuss our mutual problems. It was the last time I saw him. I found the same fresh enthusiasm, the same fighting spirit, which had struck me at Bordeaux, the same habitual kindness and a complete absence of that carping outlook which did us so much harm during the war. I don't imagine that Todaro had missed the obvious weaknesses in our wartime organization or the dangerous paralysis which gripped our strategy; but he rarely mentioned them and never dwelt on them.

In the spring of 1942 he was busy with his midget submarines to the exclusion of everything else. He tackled the job with his usual enthusiasm and, when everything was ready, transferred himself and his force overland to the Black Sea. It would be interesting to write an account of his landward navigation of tractor-borne midget submarines; but we must pass that over. I will only say that the Italian craft, based on Foros in the Yalta area, fought and sank a number of enemy ships. Todaro was always in the van either with the submarines or with the assault-boats (*barchini*)[1] with which he raised hell, as on the occasion of the feint attack which he staged at Balaclava to cover a German landing elsewhere.

Todaro returned from the Black Sea to the Mediterranean, this time in command of a detachment of *barchini*, using a steam trawler as their parent-ship. She was an odd craft for the job; but in wartime Italy everything went into the jackpot and the personnel of Special Forces were adept at finding a use for everything that floated and every device that could be turned against the enemy. Todaro's trawler was the *Cefalo*. A few months before she had been fishing in the Gulf of Taranto. Now she was fitted with cradles on deck to carry a pair of *barchini* the whole affair was camouflaged with fish nets; and she became a formidable ship of war.

The method of operation was as follows. *Cefalo* tramped

---

[1] MTM or modified speedboats. They were flat-bottomed boats with outboard motors, capable of thirty-two knots. They carried 600 lb of explosive in the bow which was fired either on impact or by water pressure. They were one-man boats. It was the pilot's job, when about 100 yards from the target, to aim the boat, lock the steering gear and drop himself into the water. Another type, the MTSM, carried a torpedo which the helmsman could fire. These were the only assault-boats used, apart from the MAS.

the Mediterranean, a dirty and innocuous piece of old junk, with a fine display of fish nets on deck. As soon as an enemy was sighted, the nets disappeared and the *barchini* slipped into the water and raced for their target. *Cefalo's* function, in fact, was to provide living-quarters for the pilots and to transport the assault boats to areas which they could not have reached under their own power.

In December 1942, Todaro was operating in the Narrows—much as one would expect, since that was then the busiest theatre of war at sea. An operation for his forces was planned against Bône, which the enemy were then using as an offensive base. It was a difficult and dangerous affair, and miscarried for reasons which there is no space to go into here. Its indirect result was the death of Todaro, one of the bravest men and most determined fighters in the Italian Navy.

It is possible, since he was not without psychic gifts, that Todaro had a premonition of the end. He told one of his officers that he felt a strange inward disturbance; but he played his part in the operation with his usual dash and persistence. On the morning of 14 December, when *Cefalo* was homeward bound, he threw himself on his bunk to snatch an hour's rest after a night of action. Fate chose that moment to intervene, hoping perhaps to catch an old warrior off his guard. Her instrument was an American aircraft, which she brought down to sea-level and aimed, so to speak, at the unprotected trawler. A burst of machinegun fire riddled the deckhouse and hit the sleeping man in the forehead. He was found with his lips still parted in a faint smile. So died Salvatore Todaro, the knight errant, a very brave and big-hearted man.

VI

Atlantic Incidents

THE two of our submarines which most resembled U-boats in their original design were *Argo* and *Velella*. They were small, built on workman-like lines without too much superstructure, and only lacked speed to make them ideally suitable for commerce raiding in the Atlantic on the German pattern.

Argo had returned from Eritrea just before the war, and was ready for sea after a short refit, when it became necessary to find a new commander. As she belonged to the Spezia flotilla, it fell to me to propose Lieut. Crepas, then second-in-command of the minelaying submarine *Micca*. He later showed himself fully up to the job both in seamanship and fighting spirit. *Argo* was among the submarines transferred to Bordeaux. The following story illustrates both the grimness of the struggle in the Atlantic and the errors that are possible in night fighting.

In the winter of 1940, *Argo* was on patrol in the North Atlantic looking for a target, when she received a signal from *Betasom* giving the position of a convoy and ordering her to attack. She set a course at once to intercept the convoy, though it was clear from their relative positions that she could not do so in under twenty-five to thirty hours at full speed. She finally reached the indicated position at night, only to find the tragic evidence of a fight that was already over. Flames lit the scene. Some ships were on fire, others sinking; wreckage of all kinds was strewn about; and the water seemed filled with survivors.

Atlantic Incidents 35

These men, even if they were picked up by lifeboats, would still be at the mercy of the sea, with little food and water and no protection against the weather.

It was a sight to wring any heart; but what could be done? It is needless to repeat that survivors could not be taken on board a small submarine, least of all one with several weeks' patrol ahead of her. Nor could there be any question of taking boats in tow in prevailing conditions in the North Atlantic.

Argo worked her way among the boats for a while, handing out food, medical stores and clothing. Then she turned back to her search for a target. It was an anxious, meticulous search, for so far we had had little success in northern waters and had come in for some caustic criticism from our German allies. *Argo* accordingly put all she had into the search; but there was no doubt that the battle—or that phase of the battle—was finally over. There was no undamaged ship in sight; even the U-boats had left the scene. Nor was there any sign of the convoy escort, which should still have been in the area, if only to search for survivors. When he was certain that he had drawn a blank, Crepas set an easterly course in search of a more promising hunting ground. No sooner had he done so than something—something moving very fast—loomed up out of the night. He guessed rather than saw that it was a destroyer, a submarine's worst enemy; but he went straight in to the attack—in the circumstances, of course, on the surface. The range was calculated in a few seconds and two torpedoes fired at the moving mass. *Argo* then withdrew at full speed and, as she did so, felt the concussion of two explosions. It was a sure hit; with two torpedoes in her belly the destroyer could confidently be written off.

But Crepas, wanting to make sure, turned back in his tracks, keeping a sharp lookout for wreckage, survivors or perhaps even a sinking ship. A long search produced nothing except, finally, a few bits of flotsam and a considerable quantity of papers and logbooks scattered over a wide area. These were gathered up and from them Crepas learnt that his victim had been H.M.C.S. *Saguenay*. As no other trace could be found, he inferred, reasonably enough, that she was a total loss and had left nothing behind except her identity card, so to speak, in the form of part of the ship's papers.

It was an important success. Crepas congratulated himself and went on with his patrol. He sank a merchantman by night on the surface after an attack initiated by his executive officer, De Santis, who was in charge of the bridge while he was getting some sleep; and then, being low in fuel, turned for home. *Argo* was almost in the Bay of Biscay when an incident occurred which threw gloom over an otherwise successful cruise. The blow came not from the enemy but from the sea, from the storm-bound Atlantic, whose violence tried our men's endurance to the utmost. A wave, steeper than usual, swept De Santis overboard. *Argo* hove to and began an intensive search, quartering the whole area without result. It was weather in which nothing could live. After twenty-four hours the search was abandoned and *Argo* returned to *Betasom*, where she was greeted with congratulations for her success and sympathy for her loss.

The next day *B.d.U* asked for a confirmation of the reportedly sunk destroyer's identity and the name *Saguenay* was repeated. But there was evidently something wrong. A few hours later we were told that *Saguenay* had been reported homeward bound to her base in Scotland. Signals flew between *Betasom* and the *B.d.U* and finally we were shown some intercepted enemy signals, from which it appeared that *Saguenay*, her bow shot away, had been taken in tow by another ship and was creeping towards the British Isles at about three knots. The next report showed her almost home and surrounded by aircraft, tugs and escorts. Alas for the claims of Crepas and the crew of the *Argo!*

It must be admitted that British ships had tough skins, if

two torpedoes were not enough to finish them. But much the same was true, on occasion, of certain Italian destroyers.

A number of men were lost overboard from our Atlantic submarines, especially during the early months. Each time it happened, the ship's company came back not only sad but somewhat disheartened, as if the loss of a man at sea, and the failure to rescue him, had struck them a collective blow. Losses by enemy action, however sad, were easier to accept; but in fact there were few single casualties. If the enemy scored a direct hit, it was generally the whole boat that went. But one such incident is worth recording, for in it the Navy lost a keen and courageous officer of an old Service family, Sub.-Lieut. Carlo Marenco Di Moriondo.

He was a young man, just out of the Naval College and fervently patriotic. He was killed in action on *Glauco* and buried at sea, where his heart was and where family tradition had led him. It was in a night action against a small, unescorted merchantman, an action which seemed insignificant at first, but proved otherwise, when *Glauco*, having missed with her torpedoes, opened fire with her guns. In most actions of the kind, the merchantman's crew abandoned ship and took to the boats, but in this case the fire was returned and not without success. Marenco, who was officer of the watch, seeing that the enemy's shots were falling close, made up his mind to bring the aftergun into action as well as the forward one, which was the only one then firing. To save time and ensure an accurate aim, he went to lay the gun himself. He ignored the enemy's well aimed fire and had, I am sure, no thought in his mind but to do his duty and make his contribution to victory. He brought his gun into action and had fired one or two rounds, when an enemy shell sprayed the deck with splinters and killed him. The brief episode was over. *Glauco* dived to escape gunfire which had now become too hot.

I said above that a total of thirty-two Italian submarines

operated in the Atlantic. So far we have only seen twenty-seven through the Straits of Gibraltar. To complete the tally we must add *Cagni* and four submarines from the Red Sea. The latter's story is well known. When Massawa was about to fall, *Guglielmotti, Ferraris, Archimede* and *Perla,* the only surviving submarines in the Red Sea, were ordered to transfer to Bordeaux by the Indian Ocean and the Atlantic. They thus avoided Gibraltar and only had to tackle the less difficult problem of the Perim passage. On the other hand, they were in a poor state of efficiency, partly as the result of twelve months in tropical waters and partly because of the isolated and increasingly precarious position of their late base. Nevertheless, all four reached their destination—though after certain adventures on the way—including the little *Perla,* classified in all naval directories as "short-range submarine." From Massawa to Bordeaux she had to cover 14,000 miles and was twice refuelled at sea by German tankers. But she got there.

Cagni's story was very different. She was built and fitted out between 1941 and 1942 expressly for ocean warfare. As soon as she was commissioned, she left the Mediterranean via Gibraltar, completed a successful patrol in which she sank three ships, and arrived safely at Bordeaux. This completes our total of thirty-four passages through the Straits.

By the summer of 1941 it had become clear to us at *Betasom* —and still more to the *B.d.U*—that, despite the alterations which had been carried out, some Italian submarines would never be fully efficient for Atlantic operations. These it was decided to repatriate. Accordingly eleven submarines were sent back to the Mediterranean that summer and again passed the Straits one by one, though this time with different and clearer orders. Ten of them made the trip successfully, bringing our total score to forty-four. The eleventh, *Glauco* (Lt. Cdr. Baroni), did not get through. But it would be wrong to attribute her loss to the passage of the Straits, for it happened in an

Atlantic Incidents

action 250 miles to the west. She was surprised on the surface by a British destroyer and dived at once. But her enemy, H.M.S. *Wishart*, had spotted her and after four hours' hunt, straddled her with a well-placed pattern of depth charges. The result, according to the oral account we had from one of the few survivors, was to spring a number of leaks in the hull, fuse the motors and damage the batteries. *Glauco* faced a problem with only two answers—to go down as she was or try a last desperate battle on the surface. She chose the second and came up. She received some hits as she surfaced, but managed to clear her own gun. Then she was swept by another burst of shell and machinegun fire; several of her crew were hit; and *Glauco* up-ended and began to sink. Further shots, probably aimed at the submarine, killed a number of men in the sea. Finally, when *Glauco* slid out of sight, *Wishart* picked up the survivors, including *Glauco's* commander.

This was our only loss in the many operations in which Italian submarines forced the Straits of Gibraltar.

VII

Torelli's Career

THE hero (or heroine) of this story is not a commander, an officer or a rating but a ship—to be more precise, a submarine. As everyone knows who has spent any time at sea, ships, though officially classed as inanimate objects, are in fact no such thing. No sailor would dare to deny that his boat has a brain, a career and a personality of her own. The same is true of a warship; and no one who fought at sea between 1940 and 1945 would think to question it. Sceptics may be referred to certain significant episodes in the Battle of Cape Matapan, about which I shall have something to say later. For the moment we can concentrate on the wartime career of one particular ship with a mind of her own—the submarine *Torelli*, whose passage through the Straits has already been described. She was one of the bravest and most faithful of Italy's submarines. She spent three eventful years in the Atlantic and then, in the summer of 1943, sailed without any fuss from Bordeaux to Singapore. In the end she found her grave in the China Sea; but it was, you may say, a natural death, for the principal characteristic of this remarkable boat was her capacity for bringing her crew safely back to port.

Torelli was very young at the outbreak of war, indeed scarcely born, for her final trials did not take place until August 1940. She would then have liked a shakedown cruise, an opportunity to find herself and test her machinery and her crew before she took to the high seas. But this was not allowed. Others did not foresee that a new submarine might like to do a little

Torelli's *Career* 41

sailing in home waters before she took on her war work in the ocean. I shall not make any comment on this policy except to say that no German submarine was considered operational until she had had three months' shakedown in the Baltic.

Torelli, on the other hand, left for the Atlantic as soon as she had run her final dockyard trials. She had a rather elderly commander, in his forties, who had not served in submarines for some time, a crew which had not yet shaken down and one officer—he joined her just as she was casting off—who had never been on board a submarine before. (He later became *Torelli's* last skipper.) Nevertheless, she negotiated the Straits, as I have described, and carried out a month's patrol off the Azores. Fate was not particularly kind to her and presented her, among other things, with a young hurricane, which caught her head-on. But she came through it all handsomely enough and arrived in Bordeaux at the beginning of October, a little battered, but having established her reputation for reaching port, whatever opposition she might meet from the enemy or the weather.

She returned to Bordeaux again in July 1942 under Bruno Migliorini's command. That time she had caught it good and proper, but she made her port nevertheless. True, it took her six weeks; but the important thing in such cases is to get there. I won't set out all her adventures in detail, which might end by being boring. But the high lights were as follows. She was bombed from the air; her batteries caught fire; she stranded on Cape Penas, in northern Spain, and got herself off and out of neutral waters within the legal time limit; she was attacked again by Sunderlands and seriously damaged; she took refuge in Santander, carried out repairs in the harbor and escaped while Spanish tugs were actually bringing her into the quay. Finally, she made Bordeaux on 15 July 1942.

As I say, she always got home. She had even managed to do so early in 1942 after a heavy and prolonged attack by ships and aircraft. She was then under Antonio De Giacomo's command, serving off the Brazilian coast, and was straddled by several sticks of bombs at a moment when, as luck would have it, she could not dive. She lost two men—Coxswain Pallucchini and Radioman Lubrano, both killed by bomb splinters while serving the A.A. gun. (They were *Torelli's* only casualties during the whole war.) But in return she shot down one aircraft and hit another and was able to finish her patrol, in the course of which she sent a tanker to the bottom. *Torelli* had previously sunk other ships while under De Giacomo's command; but her most brilliant exploit was under Primo Longobardo, who later died heroically on *Calvi*, and was posthumously awarded the Gold Cross. Between 5 January and 6 February 1941, *Torelli* was on patrol in the North Atlantic and performed the feat of entirely destroying single-handed an enemy convoy of four ships. The whole action, from the sighting of the convoy to the actual action, occupied forty-eight tense hours; but the result was one of our most conspicuous single-ship successes. On her way back to base, *Torelli* experienced the inevitable pursuit by an enemy hunting-group but, in order to finish her patrol in glory, succeeded in sinking a fifth merchantman on the way.

A brilliant action, well-conducted by a brave captain; but it was not in fighting that *Torelli* really showed at her best, as much as in patient, methodical operations of a different kind. When she had to fight, she did so with complete confidence, as she had for Longobardo and De Giacomo, but her strongest suit was getting out of difficulties which would have proved fatal to any other submarine. One can see the skill she showed under Migliorini in getting clear of the enemy and escaping internment; but the best example of all is her long and hazardous voyage from Bordeaux to Singapore under Lt. Groppallo's command—the same officer who had joined her in 1940 as she was casting off. This was *Torelli's* last voyage and one which extended over eleven weeks. But a detailed description must wait for another chapter, because it involves the adventures of other submarines and the outcome of a skillful and complex operation.

VIII

Pittoni and the *Bagnolini*

THE Italian Navy achieved its first success of the war on the night of 12 June 1940, when the submarine *Bagnolini* torpedoed the British cruiser *Calypso*. To tell the truth, this episode, which occurred less than forty-eight hours after the outbreak of war, was hardly noticed at the time, even in naval circles; and there are not many people who remember it. But it was an action in which one does not know what most to admire—the boldness and precision with which it was executed or the skill and clearheadedness of the captain, Lt. Cdr. Franco Tosoni Pittoni. I say "clearheadedness" intentionally because previously there had been a good deal of confused thinking in the Italian Navy about the possibility of night attacks by submarines. Tosoni, however, knew exactly what he was about, either by day or by night. He knew instinctively because he had been ten years in submarines and understood the potentialities of his weapon. Consequently, when one night he sighted a British cruiser squadron, he stayed on the surface and concentrated on closing the range as much as possible, despite the presence of the destroyer screen, the most deadly enemy that a submarine can have.

Bagnolini closed up in the way that one should always do, especially in a night action. When she was within a few hundred yards of the British squadron, she fired her torpedoes and dived to escape the counterattack, which developed at once. But

Tosoni, knowing his position in relation to the enemy, was certain that he could not have missed. It took about thirty seconds for the sound of the torpedoes' explosion to reach the submarine. Some days later the crew of *Bagnolini* learnt that they had sunk the *Calypso*, the first of the twelve cruisers which the British lost in the Mediterranean between June 1940 and September 1943.

For this action Tosoni was awarded the Silver Cross—one of the few cases in which the sinking of an enemy warship did not win the Gold Cross. Later, having transferred to the Atlantic with *Bagnolini*, Tosoni made a new name for himself as a commerce raider. But his most severe test came in December 1940 and was one from which he emerged with great credit, though at the cost of severe damage to his submarine. It was another proof of the exceptional gifts of seamanship and command possessed by this slightly built enthusiast, who looked even younger than he was and won the hearts of both his men and his superior officers.

All this, was in December 1940. The first intimation that *Bagnolini* was in serious trouble reached *Betasom* in the form of a cipher signal from Tosoni, in which he reported that his submarine "had damaged her batteries and was making a good deal of water; her compass was also out of order, but he had set a course to the south. . . ." At the time when this signal was received, *Bagnolini* was known to be on patrol off the south coast of England, so that her position appeared to be extremely grave, if not desperate. The only redeeming feature was the statement that she was heading south and must, therefore still have her diesels in action. She could not dive and had no electricity and no compass; but she could still move. That was something—enough, at any rate, to keep a little flicker of hope alive at *Betasom*. Moreover, Tosoni's first message did not end there. He added the information that he had sunk a merchantman, an auxiliary cruiser and, possibly, a destroyer.

It did not require much imagination to see what had happened. Tosoni had evidently attacked a convoy and sunk one merchant ship and an escort and had then faced a counterattack, all the riskier because he had chosen to pick off his victims at the very entrance to the lion's den.

At *Betasom, Bagnolini's* signal was studied at once; but there was not much help that we could give. Tosoni was ordered to try to make St. Jean-de-Luz, plotting his course as best he could. Next morning the Germans agreed to provide an escort of aircraft and M-boats;[1] and the whole southern coast of the Bay of Biscay was alerted. On the following day, the weather was so bad that the German search failed to pick up the submarine. But that night another signal was received from Tosoni to the effect that he hoped to make St. Jean-de-Luz by dawn. And it was in that small French port that I first heard the story of his adventures.

Late one afternoon he had sighted an enemy convoy and given chase. That night he attacked and scored hits with his torpedoes on two British ships, which later proved to be a merchantman and an auxiliary cruiser. So far everything had gone smoothly; then, as *Bagnolini* was disengaging, the British escort got on her tail and a hunt which lasted for a day and a night began.

Tosoni, as I have said, knew his job and had his boat well in hand. He dived deep and then, relying on his hydrophones, began a complicated pattern of maneuvers, darting this way and that and making frequent changes of speed and depth. The British destroyers stayed over *Bagnolini* the rest of the night; and by dawn they had been reinforced by aircraft. The search continued with increasing intensity all that day and the following night. Meanwhile, conditions on board *Bagnolini* had been getting steadily worse. She was making water, having sprung several rivets and opened at least one seam; and her batteries

[1] Fast minesweepers.

were flooded and were giving off chlorine. She could no longer hold her depth and had to come up to forty-five, to forty, to thirty fathoms. The lighting system had failed and her rudders were beginning to cause trouble. The end seemed very near.

But Tosoni had no intention of going down like a rat caught in a trap. It was better to surface, even under the noses of enemy destroyers, and face the unequal battle which would follow and die with some éclat, rather than prolong the slow agony below. So *Bagnolini* came up. The diesels started more quickly than they had ever done; the guns were cleared away in a few seconds and the torpedo tubes loaded. Two destroyers loomed up astern, very close, and Tosoni fired a parting salvo of four torpedoes before setting his course for the south. He had a distinct impression of having scored a hit; but the loss was never officially confirmed, so we must write it off here as a possible. There is no doubt that Tosoni's final thrust disorganized the opposition and threw them temporarily off balance, for *Bagnolini* was not attacked again, perhaps not even followed, as she made her getaway. But she was now in such straits that Tosoni despaired of bringing her home safely. This was the point at which he sent his signal. He knew well enough that he could expect little help and must rely on his own resources; but he made his signal all the same, perhaps to report his success, perhaps simply because it gave him a link with *Betasom* and so with home. He did not put it like that when he made his oral report to me; but one could read something of the kind in his expression and on the faces of the enlisted men standing around.

Bagnolini went in for repairs. Her commander, after a long leave, transferred to *Bianchi*, a newer boat, faster and better armed than *Bagnolini*. But *Bianchi* was missing on her next patrol. We know now that she was torpedoed, homeward bound in the Bay of Biscay, by the submarine *Severn* on 7 August 1941.

IX

Tramping to Singapore

Anyone who saw *Cappellini* leave La Pallice, north of Bordeaux, on 11 May 1943, would have had great difficulty in guessing that this strange floating object, heading out to sea, was really a submarine on the surface with her diesels going full speed. All that could be seen was a hump moving through the water, which only the initiated could have recognized as the bow of a submarine, and then, further aft, the outline of the bridge bristling with all the bits and pieces which a self-respecting submarine carries around with her. This would have been more easily recognizable, even without the periscopes and the aerial of the *Metox*[1] sticking up beside the loop of the direction finder. Abaft the bridge everything was under water. So was the forecastle except for the extreme point of the bows; so was the after-deck and the engine room hatch; so was the gun platform, though the gun itself had been dismounted; so were the exhausts of the diesels down which, if the engines had stopped suddenly, half the sea would have flooded.

Very few people would have recognized an Italian submarine in these two humps moving slowly through the waters of La Pallice. Still less would they have thought that the submarine was sailing at her full surface speed and with the intention of covering 13,000 miles in this extraordinary trim across two oceans entirely dominated by the enemy. But this marine phe-

---

[1] An apparatus which showed the presence of radar operating in the area.

nomenon was in fact *Cappellini*, stuffed like a crocodile, with an odd assortment of cargo and under orders to sail from the west coast of France to Sabang in Sumatra, and thence to Singapore, exactly halfway round the world.

In all, seven submarines were earmarked for this difficult voyage, carrying much-needed materials to our Japanese ally, and returning with an equally valuable cargo for our own war industry. But of the seven, only five actually started. *Cappellini* was the first to leave and, as we shall see, made a record trip. She was followed by *Tazzoli* on 16 May; *Giuliani* on 23 May; *Torelli* on 14 June; and *Barbarigo* on 15 June. Five Italian submarines sailing under German names—*Cappellini* became *Adler 3*—because the operation was a German one, though the commanders and crews were all Italian. On their arrival in the Far East our boats were to report to *Eritrea*, an Italian sloop which, under Iannucci's, command, had slipped out of Massawa in 1941 for Indonesia, under the noses of British cruisers and Dutch aircraft, eluding the former by a little luck and more skill, and deceiving the latter by the judicious use of a few cans of paint and a dummy mast. On 8 September 1943 the same ship, in obedience to orders, waved good-by to the Malayans, Japanese and Germans at Singapore and, taking advantage of rainstorms and fog, ran the Straits of Malacca at the speed of ten knots and emerged undetected in the Indian Ocean.

Between May and June 1943, as I said, five Italian submarines, converted from warships into slow and inoffensive merchantmen, left the French coast. Only three—Auconi's *Cappellini*, Groppallo's *Torelli* and Tei's *Giuliani*—reached their destination. *Tazzoli* and *Barbarigo*, two names famous in our submarine history, never made Sabang or any other port, but were lost without trace like so many of their fellows. Even today, after consulting British and American records, no one knows exactly when or how they were lost. *Tazzoli* is

Tramping to Singapore 49

thought to have been sunk by a British aircraft in the Bay of Biscay on 16 June, the day she left the Gironde; but the loss of *Barbarigo* remains a mystery. Perhaps she was sunk by aircraft, perhaps by another submarine, which later disappeared herself; perhaps, since anything is possible, she was simply lost at sea.

The idea of using Italian submarines for blockade-running between Europe and the Far East originated, so far as I know, at *Betasom*, when the then Captain of Submarines, Capt. Enzo Grossi, reluctantly decided that the seven submarines still at Bordeaux were no longer fit for commerce raiding. Grossi so reported to Admiral Doenitz in February 1943, adding his opinion that to go on using them in this way was to send them to certain death. He asked instead if he could put Italian crews into seven of the new German U-boats. This was not such an odd request as it sounds, for the Germans, who were then launching one U-boat a day, were short of crews, whereas we had a surplus of crews for the boats we still possessed or were able to build.

Doenitz agreed with Grossi's proposal at once, but made the stipulation that *Betasom* should convert the Italian submarines at Bordeaux into cargo boats for use between Axis-controlled Europe and the Far East. There was a vital need for traffic of this kind, for the Japanese were desperately short of mercury, alloy-steel and medical stores, which Germany and Italy could supply, while the Axis was equally short of Far Eastern tin, cotton and rubber.

In the conditions existing in 1943 it was no longer possible to use ordinary merchant ships. In the two previous years some Italian motor-ships, of which I shall say more, had succeeded in running the blockade with mercury and arms for Japan, cotton and rubber for Europe. But after the arrival of *Orseolo* at Bordeaux in the spring of 1943, no other merchant ship had been able to risk the voyage. Consequently, if any trade were to be carried on at all, it had to be by submarines, which could, if necessary, escape the enemy's attention by submerging.

This was the origin of the deal by which Germany handed over seven efficient U-boats to Italian crews and we in exchange converted our remaining submarines—still manned and commanded by Italians—to cargo boats on the Far Eastern run. The agreement was, of course, scrupulously honored on both sides. *Betasom* sent off her boats to Singapore as and when they were ready; and Doenitz, on his side, regularly shipped Italian crews in the U-boats under orders for Bordeaux. In fact, on 8 September, these ex-German submarines were just about to sail for their new base, while *Bagnolini* and *Finzi*, the last boats of the Atlantic Flotilla, with their cargo on board, were on the point of leaving for Singapore. But then the Armistice intervened and cancelled all plans.

Let me say at once that submarines make unsatisfactory cargo boats; but so would any warship or anything else, for that matter, which was used for a purpose for which it was not designed. To make the point clear, I must explain that the maximum cargo which could possibly be crammed into the largest of these converted submarines was 150 tons on the outward voyage and 190 tons on the homeward voyage, which did not in fact take place. How small a cargo this was can be seen by making a comparison with an ordinary small merchantman, or tramp, which would normally carry 3,000 or 4,000 tons.

The 190 tons loaded by *Giuliani* at Singapore for her homeward voyage was an outside limit, only made possible because she expected to refuel at sea. The normal cargo was 120 to 150 tons or even as little as 95 tons, which was all that *Cappellini* succeeded in loading at La Pallice. True, it was a valuable cargo of alloy-steel, mercury in bottles and cases of munitions, but still only 95 tons. To illustrate the point I will add the list of what *Cappellini* took on board at Singapore: 92 tons of rubber; 54 of tin; 5 of tungsten; 4 of opium and quinine—a total of 155 tons with rather less fuel than on the outward voyage because, like *Giuliani*, she expected to refuel at sea.

I have already said that in these cargo-carrying submarines the guns were dismounted. In fact, the whole armament was stripped, partly to make room for more cargo, partly so as to remove any temptation which the skippers might have had to fight. Their job was to carry their 100 tons of cargo to the other side of the world—that and nothing else. If they met an American aircraft-carrier or an English troopship, they were to let them go, without even reporting their positions, because at that moment tin, mercury and rubber were more important than all the aircraft carriers and troopships in the world.

The only guns left on board were the A.A. machine-guns on the bridge, and they were of little use against the big, long-range British and American aircraft. All the other armament had been removed, torpedoes put on shore, ammunition lockers converted to fuel tanks (with the inevitable result of oil leaks inside the submarine) and torpedo tubes turned into storage space. One section of batteries had also been removed, so that the boats' speed and handiness under water were much reduced. Every inch of space that could be found was crammed with cargo, extra fuel or stores. Bunks disappeared and so did the cubbyhole dignified on submarines by the name of captain's cabin. Two of the lavatories were scrapped, leaving only one for the whole crew, and with them went everything which could be classed as a comfort—showers, cupboards, locker space, etc. It is difficult to visualize how much room can be taken up by 95 tons of cargo, 260 tons of fuel and food and fresh water for 50 men for three months—for even men who are prepared to work under the most difficult conditions still have to be kept alive.

The result was chaotic. Men slept squeezed between a case of sphaghetti and a bottle of mercury; the electric stove was mounted on a pile of canned vegetables; and the bars of alloy steel were used as a platform from which to inspect the hydraulic gear.

Torelli had an additional problem of her own in the shape of a passenger—the Japanese Lt. Col. Kinze Saterke, who was going home after learning all that the Germans could teach him about radio. He brought seven suitcases with him, as mysterious as they were large, which evidently contained top secret documents and apparatus, for he refused to be parted from them during the whole of an adventurous two months' voyage.

Enemy aircraft and destroyers made a dead set at *Torelli*. They were on top of her from the moment she poked her nose out of Bordeaux and did not let go until she had passed St. Helena. The original team from the British Isles handed her on to another from Gibraltar, and that team to one from the Azores, supported by partners from Cape Verde. Then came destroyers, corvettes and every kind of mischief from Freetown, from Ascension and finally from St. Helena itself. But *Torelli* was a remarkable submarine with a particular gift for shaking off corvettes, frigates, Sunderlands and Catalinas. She lived up to her reputation once more and was able to show the Japanese colonel how an unarmed Italian submarine out of trim and very unhandy when submerged, could still defy a fierce and systematic hunt. She had, of course, to take an evasive route, spend several days longer at sea than she had intended and, what was worse, exceed her estimated fuel consumption by a fairly wide margin. As the result, she ran out of fuel in the middle of the Indian Ocean, despite the extra load she was carrying and all the care taken to keep consumption down. If she reached Sabang at all, it was only because she fell in with a German U-boat from whom she was able to take on enough fuel to make port. And so *Torelli* reached Sumatra with her Japanese colonel and his secret papers, her steel ingots, bottles of mercury and a few gun-mountings.

Let us now return to *Cappellini*, whom we left pulling out

of the little harbor of La Pallice with no more than her bridge and the tip of her bow showing out of the water. Her engine room telegraph indicated full speed ahead; but, given her weight and trim, full speed meant something between six and seven knots at most. In this state she reached the open sea just in time to catch an air attack, the first of a long and weary series.

In the early part of the war a submarine attacked from the air, if well-armed and under good control, usually stayed on the surface and fought it out with her opponent. But by the summer of 1943, I doubt if any submarine commander would have had the slightest wish to engage in action with the aircraft that were flapping around him. There were too many of them for one thing, and all their vital parts were well armored; for another, they were equipped with a gyroscopic bomb sight, which made it almost impossible to miss. For a submarine as badly armed as *Cappellini* and only floating by a miracle, to have accepted battle would have been practically suicide, so Auconi ordered a crash dive.

I should now go into complicated explanations to show why a submarine, which is already down by the stern, cannot dive as quickly as she should; but it is better to skip technicalities. What cannot be skipped, however, is the stream of water which found its way in through a weak joint as soon as *Cappellini* reached a certain depth. Nor can we pass over the cargo, which shifted all over the place as soon as her fore and aft trim was altered. When that sort of thing happens ordinarily, one blows a ballast tank and everything returns to normal. But *Cappellini* was carrying a minimum of ballast to make more room for fuel and cargo and, if she had got rid of any of it, her bridge and her bow would have broken surface again. To get back onto an even keel, she had to bring some of her crew forward and keep her pumps going furiously. Meanwhile, the men on duty at the various wheels, levers and switches, the vent-and-blow panel and the telemotor gear had to climb over mountains of cases, boxes and bottles and sometimes even to crawl on all fours through the mass of gear which littered the boat from end to end in order to reach their posts and carry out the orders they received.

I have taken this account from Auconi's report. He also remarks that it was like this throughout the whole voyage. The quantity of cargo never grew any less, but the pile of stores gradually sank, so that it became possible to stow the remainder more conveniently. They were even able to give the spaces a bit of an airing when they surfaced, though the hatches, which were never above water, still remained closed.

Cappellini escaped her first air attack by diving and took care of all the others in the same way. These followed one another in a monotonous series from the Bay of Biscay to the latitude of Madeira. *Giuliani* and *Torelli* encountered much the same difficulties but were both lucky enough to come through successfully. Since they were larger, problems of control and stowage were probably less serious than on *Cappellini;* but the difficulties of navigation were the same for everyone, so that in this respect the three captains' reports duplicated each other.

There was one slight difference in that *Torelli,* as we have seen, had Colonel Kinze on board, while *Giuliani,* apart from the steel and mercury, carried the personal baggage of the Japanese Embassy in Paris. But this neither increased nor diminished Commander Tei's problems, which he solved quite satisfactorily by bringing his boat into Sabang, sixty days out from Bordeaux. This was a few days more than *Cappellini* and a few less than *Torelli.* For the rest, all three had much the same adventures and mishaps. They all suffered the same air attacks night and day, in fog, rain or fine weather, on the surface or submerged, while they were sailing or while they were charging batteries. They all tried to find an answer to the question. Is it better to sail on the surface during the day and submerge at night or the other way round? I don't believe there is any final answer. The ideal solution would have been to have dived deep as they came out of port and surfaced again somewhere in the South Atlantic. But for submarines not equipped with *Schnorkels,* as ours weren't, that was impractical. In fact, if they wanted to complete their trip on time, they could not afford to submerge too often, since their under-water speed was not much more than three knots. They were obliged, of course, to go down during the more dangerous sections of their route; but otherwise it was a case of running on the surface under the diesels at an economic cruising speed.

The real difficulty lay in deciding what were the more dangerous sections of the route. The whole voyage was one long risk, at least as far south as St. Helena. Then came another bad stretch off Capetown, which the persistency of the South Africans made one of the nastiest sections of the whole route. I doubt, in fact, whether this combativeness did the Allies much good; but it caused *Betasom* to order our submarines to keep at least 300 miles clear of the Cape. Some of them obeyed; others did not. One of the latter was *Cappellini.* As soon as she realized that her fuel was only just going to last out, she decided to cut the distance to a minimum by keeping close in to the coast. Accordingly, she scraped past Madeira, inviting the inevitable air attack and a hunt by British corvettes from the Cape Verde Islands and Freetown. Then, sailing partly on the surface and partly submerged, she reached the Equator unscathed, thanks to a good deal of luck and some cover from a tropical rainstorm. "A symbolic douche of sea water," says the log, "for those who had not crossed the Line before and a non-symbolic douche of bombs from aircraft probably out of Ascension. On 13 June we were off Cape Town, passing less than forty miles from that base."

The orders said three hundred miles; but it was a good thing that *Cappellini* ignored them, for she reached Sabang with no more than two hours' fuel remaining.

There was a time in the days of coal-fired boilers and before Pullino[1] had thought of submarines, when a captain who found himself short of fuel could give the traditional order to burn the cabin furniture or even the woodwork of the bridge and thus bring his ship happily into port. But on *Cappellini* it would have been difficult to persuade the diesels to digest aluminium furniture or iron deck plates. Since there was nothing on hand but the oil in the reserve tanks, Auconi managed very well. So, for that matter, did Tei in *Giuliani*, who only just made it by following the prescribed route, a fact which did not prevent him from running into a heavy attack, southwest of Madeira, from a flight of aircraft which pounced on him out of a fogbank.

At this point I may remind any reader who has forgotten that by 1943 all British and American aircraft operating on the high seas or in the Mediterranean were equipped with radar, which could spot a submarine on the surface at a range of fifty miles, and, of course, worked just as well at night, in the thickest fog or the heaviest tropical rainstorm. The submarine, on the other hand, had no warning of the flock of birds of ill-omen who were about to swoop on her. Or rather, she had eyes when she could use them—that is, on a clear day—the *Metox*. This instrument was supposed to give warning when radar was in use in the area; but it sometimes failed to work and, worse still, was itself detectable on a radar screen.

Off the Cape, *Cappellini* struck a westerly gale—one of the kind which keep aircraft in their hangars and corvettes in harbor with their mooring lines doubled. It put the old boat to a very severe test. Auconi reported afterwards that they had been fortunate in having a following sea. No doubt he was speaking relatively, for he added: "The whole of the after-deck, including the engine exhausts, carried away. Men on safety-lines worked feverishly, with seas constantly breaking over them, to

---

[1] Giacinto Pullino (1831-1897), Piedmontese engineer, who built the first Italian submarine, the *Delfino*.

Admiral Parona and the author (right) at Bordeaux.

Admiral Doenitz inspects Italian crews at Bordeaux.

An Italian submarine attacks a British tanker.

alian submarine Malaspina *sinks* British Fame.

Armed merchantman torpedoed by Italian submarine.

Italian submarine and U-boat meet on the high seas.

Torpedo boat Circe *sinks British submarine* Temp

cut away loose plates which were threatening to intensify the damage already done. Then the gale increased and became almost more than we could stand. We were taking water right over the bridge and down the hatch, which was the only air intake for the diesels. More water was coming into the control room than the pumps could deal with. This continued for over a week. We carried out repairs as best we could, partly on the surface and partly submerged. At a depth of forty fathoms we had a ten-degree roll. Diving and surfacing were delicate operations and obviously dangerous, especially as the batteries were swashing over large quantities of acid."

I have given this extract in full because there are times when bald, official prose is worth any amount of fine writing. I need only add that, after a month at sea, life on board was better organized than when *Cappellini* set out, if only because the oil in the torpedo tubes and ammunition lockers had been used up and a good quantity of stores consumed. Consequently there was more room to move about and one could do so without getting covered with oil. On the other hand, a certain amount of sea water had inevitably reached the batteries, where it was generating chlorine gas, most of which ended in the crew's lungs, since the forward and the after hatch were still under water and the ventilating system was behaving in a very unorthodox way. By 20 June *Cappellini* was in the Indian Ocean, having crossed the Atlantic from north to south at a time when the U-boats were suffering their worst losses of the whole war and Italy was reporting the submarines *Morosini*, *Archimede* and *Da Vinci* as missing. On 9 July she entered the port of Sabang in Sumatra, where she was greeted by *Eritrea* and by the Japanese Lt. Cdr. Yoshida, locally known as the King of Sabang. Three weeks later *Giuliani* arrived and on 26 August *Torelli*. All three were immediately taken in to Singapore by *Eritrea* to unload their cargoes, carry out necessary repairs and re-load and revictual for the homeward voyage.

At this ex-British base—captured intact by the Japs, who found enormous stocks of food, fuel and munitions—endless discussions went on between the Italian Commander Iannucci, the Japanese Admiral Enamoto, the German Von Zatorsky and the skippers of the three submarines. One party wanted to mark time, the other to hurry up the turn round. In the end only *Cappellini* was ready to sail by the beginning of September with a fine cargo of 155 tons of rubber, tin, quinine and opium, together with as much fuel as would take her to the point in the South Atlantic where she had a rendezvous with a U-boat for refuelling. But even *Cappellini* never left the Far East.

When the Armistice came on 8 September, she was at Sabang just about to leave. *Giuliani* and *Torelli*—the latter having arrived a bare week before—were still at Singapore, loading and refitting. All three were interned and then, when their Italian crews had been marched off to a camp, were taken over by the Germans. *Giuliani*, already the *Adler 5*, was re-christened *U(IT)23* and was lost on 14 February 1944, when the British submarine *Tallyho* torpedoed her in the Malacca channel. *Torelli* and *Cappellini* were later handed over to the Japanese by the Germans when they too began to feel the pinch. Their end came when the Americans sank them off Kobe in the autumn of 1945.

Part 2. ADVENTURES IN UNIFORM

X

Invading Crete

From Bordeaux I was transferred to Leros in the Ægean. To tell the truth, my job at *Betasom* had never really appealed to me and I had been pressing for an active command. By that I did not mean the command of an island in the Ægean, but a seagoing billet, preferably in destroyers. But the Admiralty having decided otherwise, I had no choice but to obey. Accordingly, I set off by air for Leros, or rather for Rhodes, because it was some time before I got as far as Leros itself. You will see why in a moment. But first I must say something about the flight from Italy to the Dodecanese, partly because of an incident which occurred on the way, partly because the first pilot of the aircraft was my brother Enzo, a major in the Air Force Reserve.

Enzo, a veteran of the air, had been a civil pilot and was recalled at the outbreak of the war with the rank of captain. His first job was to fly the three-engined transports which were ferrying dismantled fighter-aircraft from Rome to Asmara. It was a long and dangerous route, three-quarters of which lay across enemy territory. For this work Enzo was promoted and given the Silver Cross. During 1942 and 1943 he worked hard —indeed, over-worked—flying supplies to our forces in Libya, Tunis and Pantelleria. He was able to carry out all his assignments successfully, but in the process badly overstrained his heart. When he took up intensive flying again in 1950 it would no longer stand the strain and finally gave out while he was flying as captain of one of *Alitalia's* four-engined aircraft.

At the time of which I am speaking, he was on the regular service between Italy and the Ægean, so it was not difficult for me to arrange to fly with him. As it was years since we had had the chance of spending a few hours together, accident and our respective careers having kept us apart, the meeting was more than a pleasure to both of us. The plane's second pilot was Lt. Col. Fortunato Federici, another much-decorated veteran. He was later killed in action in the Ægean, over the island of Amorgos, at the end of 1941.

We were flying over the Corinth Canal—incidentally a prohibited area—and were all very happy, when, about noon on 20 May 1941, we sighted a heavy formation of German aircraft, escorted by fighters. Our course was easterly, while they were heading south, so we soon left them behind, without any of us being able to guess what their destination was. The incident did nothing to disturb our enjoyment of the flight, which went on as calmly and peacefully as a pleasure trip. We landed on schedule at the airport of Gadurra in Rhodes in the late afternoon; and here we found the answer to the problem which had puzzled us on the way. It was D-day for the German attack on Crete. The planes we had seen were carrying the assault troops to Maleme and Retimo airfields on the western end of the island.

Everyone remembers that it was a bitterly contested operation. What is often forgotten is that an Italian sea-borne expedition also took part. It landed in eastern Crete on 28 May; and it was thanks to this landing that the Germans later handed over to us the control of that end of the island. Please do not smile at the memory of this little operation. It is true that the convoy which sailed from Rhodes on the afternoon of 27 May looked more like a Walt Disney film than a highly organized amphibious force. Indeed, I doubt whether a stranger assortment of floating objects ever set out to attack a strongly fortified island across seas which, despite the activities of our aircraft, were still dominated by the enemy. But it was not a joke. The little argosy reached its destination under the noses of a British squadron; and the 500 seamen and 2,500 troops on board were landed safely and occupied the corner of Crete between Sitia, San Nicola and Hierapetra. Even the four hundred pestiferous mules which accompanied the expedition reached land safely, with one exception. This mule was thrown overboard with the rest off Sitia—our methods of disembarkation may have been rather crude—but refused to swim ashore, setting a northerly course instead, perhaps with the idea of returning to his stable in Rhodes. We also landed the expedition's stores—five days' rations and ammunition—part of which was dumped at Sitia, while the rest followed the troops by sea as they moved westward from their landing point.

What more do you want?

I agree that there were no startling deeds of valor during the voyage and that no one won the Gold Cross. But there are times when the truest courage is not to fight, if fighting means inevitable and total destruction. That was roughly our position; nevertheless, we defeated, if only in the sense of eluding a British cruiser squadron which would have swallowed us whole if they had caught us. And that was what mattered. Of course, we should have been the first to admit, the fact that everything went off perfectly was largely a matter of luck—something to offset the many times when luck had run the other way.

At this point I must go back again to the beginning. It is not necessary to re-tell the story of the German invasion of Crete; but the reader must be reminded that between 21 and 25 May the German air-borne troops were only just holding their initial positions around the airfields of Retimo, Maleme and Heraklion. In the meanwhile the two convoys, carrying the sea-borne supporting force, had been destroyed or dispersed by British ships, despite the great courage displayed by the escorting destroyers, *Lupo* and *Sagittario*. It was at this point that our authorities in Rhodes began to play with the idea, which had been in their minds since the beginning, of taking part in the operation with an Italian brigade.

Since an Italian air-borne assault was out of the question, the plan from the outset was for a landing from the sea. True, we did not then possess any specialized landing-craft, either in the Ægean or anywhere else; but this was in 1941, when some romance still hung about the war and men were supposed to be able to triumph over machines. The authorities in the Dodecanese thought, perhaps, that we were still living in the days of Garibaldi. At any rate, the miscellaneous collection of boats mentioned above was all that they considered necessary to transport a military force across the Ægean. As it turned out, they were right. The little boats did their duty and reached their destination. But I must add that this was not the result generally expected at the time, if one may judge from a certain reluctance in making local craft available. We were not permitted to use the tug, *Apuania*, for fear she would be lost. His Excellency, the Governor, would not permit us to use his *Lepanto* for the same reason. We were also refused the old *Caboto*, then stationed at Rhodes, because she was still carried on the Navy's books as a cruiser and no one wanted the enemy to be able to claim the loss of such an important ship, if the expedition miscarried.

In fact, these three ships would have been very useful: the first for her carrying capacity, the second for her guns and the third for her efficient radio apparatus. But they all had to be

Invading Crete

left in port; and the expedition's commander—handsomely styled for the occasion, Naval Commander in Chief—had to be content with a few fishing boats, a couple of tugs and so on. When they had been assembled, he drew up the following list for the benefit of future historians:

4 motor fishing vessels (*gazolini*): *Sant 'Antonio, Navigatore, Plutone* and *San Giorgio.* Splendid names, but maddeningly slow boats.

2 steamships: *Orsini* and *Tarquinia.* Good, but very small; *Orsini* carried the C. in C.'s colors.

1 river-boat, *Porto di Roma.* She came from the Tiber and had been transformed into a tank landing craft, no less.

2 refrigerator ships: *Addis Ababa* and *Assab.* Tiny and with quite useless holds.

1 lagoon steamer: *Giampaolo.* Anyone who has been to Venice will know what that means.

2 tugs: *Aguglia* and *Impero.*

3 tankers: *Nera* and two others, which were little more than gasoline lighters of the kind normally used in harbor.

Fifteen boats in all with a speed of between six and nine knots and none of the equipment necessary for landing on an enemy coast. The fishing boats and tankers had indeed been fitted with patent ramps, which the inventor fondly believed could be used for landing; but as they were unable to get near enough to the beach, their ramps remained sadly hanging from the bows, while the troops, if they wanted a dry landing, had to use the motorboats, dinghies and whaleboats which we had fortunately towed from Rhodes to Sitia.

Please do not misunderstand me. The frivolous statements I have made so far do not take away from the importance of the operation or detract from the courage of those who took part in it, well aware of the risks they were running. Yet our greatest difficulty was to persuade a few people to stay behind in Rhodes; and, even so, at the last moment we found that we had a number of stowaways.

The force embarked on our fifteen little ships was made up

of men of the 9th Infantry Division, supported by the thirteen light tanks (very light, I thought) in the *Porto di Roma*, some Blackshirt detachments (among whom I remember Terragni, the mayor of Como) and a company of Carabinieri. The C.O., Col. Caffaro, had at his disposal two cars, a small truck and the four hundred mules already mentioned—our supply services could hardly be called mechanized. Under the Naval Commander came two companies of seamen, whose task was to establish and defend the base while the infantry and "A.F.V.'s" rumbled into the interior.

So much for the preparations for our amphibious operation. As for its execution, I think I have said already that we sailed from Rhodes on the late afternoon of 27 May. Nothing of note happened that night except that there was a fresh northwesterly wind and enough swell to empty the rations out of the Infantry and Blackshirts. Next day was fine and calm and everything returned to normal. When the fleet-destroyer *Crispi*, the escorts *Lira*, *Lince* and *Libra*, two E-boats and a few fighters formed up around the convoy, the C. in C. began to feel that Nelson, dashing for the West Indies after Villeneuvre, had little on him. No doubt it was this idea which suggested to him that he might abandon his prescribed route altogether and set a course direct for Sitia, whose half-dozen houses were his final goal. The original route had been worked out with the idea of keeping the convoy close to land so that, if anything went wrong, the troops wolld at least have a reef to hang on to. This was a good idea in itself, but one which was bound to waste a good deal of time; and it was for this reason that our neo-Nelson decided to forget about island and reefs and head straight out to sea. It was fortunate that he did so because, as we shall see, it was precisely the few hours saved by the new course which enabled him to bring his command safely to Sitia.

At 1300 hours on 28 May the log of the little flagship read "Nothing to report." Under the circumstances it was the best

Invading Crete 65

and most hopeful entry that there could have been. Until 1300 hours, therefore, all was well; but then a signal from Rhodes changed our "All Clear," if not into "All Wrong," at least to something pretty near it. The signal informed us baldly that three cruisers and six destroyers of the British Navy had been sighted in the Eastern Mediterranean on course for the Ægean at full speed. They were heading, to be exact, for the straits between Crete and the island of Caxo, which we were due to cross within the next few hours. It was our reconnaissance planes which had reported the British ships, and, since their names are now known, they may as well be given. They were the cruisers *Orion*, *Ajax* and *Dido*, and the destroyers *Decoy*, *Jackal*, *Hotspur*, *Kimberley*, *Imperial* and *Hereward*, Rear Admiral Rawlings commanding. Three cruisers and six destroyers—not bad for fifteen small boats escorted by *Crispi*, three escort-destroyers and two E-boats. But to tell the truth, Admiral Rawlings was not after the 9th Infantry. His only object was to reach the north side of Crete and give support to the British troops who were still holding out. But you know how these things go. If the Admiral had happened to meet, right across his path, a number of fishing boats and gasoline lighters bulging with troops, he would certainly have improved the occasion with a little target practice.

On board *Orsini* we plotted our own and the enemy's position on the chart; and even a blind man could see that the British ships, if they continued as they were going, would be off Sitia by 1700 hours. No one objected to that in principle, but it happened to be the precise moment which we had selected for our own arrival. What could be done? We were already sailing at the maximum speed of the slowest ships in the convoy—some of the very slowest had even dropped behind. We were taking the shortest route; and we had the largest escort which our forces in the Ægean could supply. We could, of course, have turned to port and run for the island of Scarpanto, which was not far away. But the war, as I said before, was still in its romantic phase. We therefore held our course for Sitia without bothering too much about the presence of *Orion*, *Ajax* and the rest. And in fact, though we did not know this at the time, we were steadily gaining on them, thanks to the activities of the German and Italian airforces in the Ægean.

In the event, the C. in C. proved to have been right to trust to luck and everything worked out well, as the following rather scrambled entries from *Orsini's* log will show:

1330 hrs. Ordered all boats to increase speed. This made a lot of smoke without raising our speed by as much as half a knot. Tug *Impero* a long way behind.

1500 hrs. Admiral signals from Rhodes suggesting we increase speed. We had thought of this already.

1515 hrs. Ordered escort *Lince* to take *Impero* in tow and bring her up with us. *Lince* disappeared over horizon and was seen no more.

1545 hrs. *Crispi* also disappears, having received orders from Rhodes to shell the lighthouse on Cape Sidero.

1600 hrs. Learn from intercepted signals that German-Italian aircraft have attacked enemy squadron. But indicated position suggests that they have not reduced speed.

1615 hrs. Entering Sitia Bay. Two of our escorts leave us under orders from Rhodes, but *Crispi* rejoins.

1650 hrs. Opening the beach. No reaction from on shore; village apparently deserted. I order all boats in to the beach.

1700 hrs. Boats of the convoy beach themselves as instructed. *Giampaolo*—lagoon steamer carrying some three hundred men—ties up at the wooden wharf by the quay. *Crispi* stands by to beat down any opposition with her 4-inch guns; but everything still quiet on shore. Tanks from the *Porto di Roma* clamber down the ramps and occupy covering positions ashore. Seamen from the leading-parties go ashore and are ordered to rig temporary jetties, man the ship's boats which we have towed with us, and organize a ferry-service.

1720 hrs. All 3,000 men of the expeditionary force are ashore and starting their march inland. Unloading of stores begins.

Invading Crete 67

While all this was going on, the British squadron found itself in a most awkward position. Their difficulties lasted for two or three hours and slowed them down a good deal more than either Admiral Rawlings or Sir Andrew Cunningham, who commanded the Mediterranean Fleet from Alexandria, could have foreseen. It appears from Sir Andrew's memoirs—a reliable source—that *Orion* was under heavy air attack during the whole afternoon of the 28th; *Ajax* was hit by Italian torpedo-bombers of the 281th Squadron and obliged to turn back; and the destroyer *Imperial* was also attacked by a formation of S.84 bombers. Despite this, Admiral Rawlings held on his course, though at reduced speed. Between 2100 and 2200 hours he was at last off Sitia, probing the coast with searchlights and gunfire for something which was indeed there, though he failed either to find or to hit it. We can only be grateful to him, as also for the fact that he did not waste much time over these tedious evolutions under our noses. His object, as I said before, was not to pursue Italian landing parties, but to evacuate the British garrison; and with this in view he presently made off to the west after firing a few rounds in our direction and into Mirabella Bay.

By dawn next day, however, cruisers and destroyers were once again off Sitia and again under air attack, this time by Stukas, one of which dropped a bomb down the destroyer *Hereward*'s funnel and broke her in two. After this the British went off for good, leaving our E-boats to pick up the survivors. But even their return journey was not free of trouble. The air attacks continued on their way back to Alexandria and resulted —again according to Cunningham—in serious damage to the destroyer *Decoy* and then in succession to the cruisers *Dido* and *Orion*. In all, of the nine ships which left Egypt on the evening of 27 May, only three—the destroyers *Jackal, Hotspur* **and** *Kimberley*—returned undamaged.

As soon as they had landed, Col. Caffaro's infantry and tanks fanned out and occupied positions on the hills surrounding Sitia Bay. This was obviously the right course. The two companies of seamen remained behind in the deserted village, where they set up the nucleus of a supply base and took over various suitable buildings as stores. It was not a very grand affair. Everything was on a modest scale as befitted the poor relations which we were and remained throughout the war. But it was necessary to organize some sort of base, through which supplies could flow in from Rhodes; and for the moment the most convenient point to do so was the beach on which we had landed. Most of the seamen were assigned to the defense of the perimeter. The remainder, with a few officers landed from the ships, became what could be called (with a little imagination) Naval Headquarters, Crete. The commanding officer was *Betasom's* late chief of staff. He had with him Lt. Pucci as second-in-command; Lt. Sanguinetti in charge of the beach and the naval landing-parties; Aiello as port-captain; and Lt. Montanari as quartermaster. The last named had the biggest job, for it fell to him to issue rations and stores to the five hundred men who remained at Sitia.

A field bank was set up, against the time when currency should reach us and an invitation issued to the inhabitants to return home with the promise that no one would hurt them. Gradually those who had taken to the hills on our arrival filtered back, at first rather diffidently, then more trustfully and finally with complete confidence as they discovered that Italians, even when disguised as invaders, could never manage to look very fierce. With that the story of our landing in Crete is really over. The enemy's furious resistance died away rapidly[1] and ceased altogether within a few days of our landing at Sitia. The

---

[1] The decision to evacuate Crete was taken on 27 May, the day when the Italian expedition left Rhodes. (Tr.)

Italian brigade, moving from the east, made contact with the Germans at the junction of the San Nicola-Hierapetra-Heraklion roads and then took over San Nicola while the Germans occupied Hierapetra. Our base at Sitia was also transferred to San Nicola and remained there until the end of the war. Its original C.O. who was replaced by Commander Giuseppe Orlando then continued his interrupted journey to Leros by seaplane.

XI

The Attack That Failed

THE more one thinks of the defense of Tobruk against the British attack on the night of 13 September 1942, the more one admires the cool heads of the commanders, who were able to do so much with a handful of men and a few motor barges.

Improvization is an over-worked word. If I must use it here, it is only in the sense that a chronic shortage of equipment obliged Italian forces to improvize throughout the war, even in the most carefully planned operations. In this particular case, General Giannantoni, the fortress commander, had worked out elaborate plans for the defense of Tobruk. But—a "but" familiar to all Italians who served in the war—these plans depended on the existence of a number of men, guns and vehicles that were not forthcoming either in or near Tobruk. Consequently, when the British attack came, it was improvization rather than a well-thought-out tactical plan which defeated it.

It was not an easy problem, for the fortress came under simultaneous attack from land, sea and air, by sea-borne troops, by Commandos and by the Long Range Desert Group, of which Lord Montgomery was so justly proud. Let me add in parentheses that Montgomery's book, *Alamein to the Sangro*, contains no mention at all of this bold operation, of which, had it been successful, so much might have been said . . . so many things in a vein with which we are all familiar. But the attack failed disastrously—a circumstance which may have contributed to his lordship's forgetfulness. Or is it possible that he knew nothing about it?[1]

The fact remains that the British operational plan, seized from a prisoner, showed that the raid had been planned in meticulous detail and with a knowledge of the ground which suggested the careful staff work of a higher command. I can only infer from this that the 8th Army Commander was not so much in the dark as one would suppose from reading his book. But that is a point of minor importance. What matters is that the plan had foreseen everything—the demolitions to be carried out in the harbor; the ships to be sunk; the use to be made of the coastal batteries; the exact routes of the various assault parties; the capture of the motor barges, which were to be used to transport released British prisoners; even the disagreeable fate of the Italian command. Everything, as I said, had been foreseen except for the negligible possibility that the Italians might show fight. But that was precisely what happened in the early hours of 14 September. Between 1 a.m., when the attack started, and 6 a.m., when the last of the British landing force were rounded up, the outcome of the operation was decided, in a very different way from what British G.H.Q. had expected.

A few days before the attack, General Giannantoni, commanding the troops in Tobruk, had been taken to the hospital in Bardia and the command had devolved on Colonel Battaglia. The Senior Naval Officer at the port was Captain Temistocle D'Aloja; but it so happened that the C. in C. Libya, Admiral Giuseppe Lombardi, was also in Tobruk at the time and thus became the senior officer present. When it became clear that a major attack was in progress, the two local commanders joined the Admiral and a combined headquarters was formed. It was

---

[1] Planning for a raid on Tobruk to relieve pressure on the 8th Army was initiated by General Auchinleck, C. in C. Middle East, early in August. His successor, General Alexander, approved the final plan in September. A copy was also sent to General Montgomery, the new 8th Army Commander, who did not comment as he was not directly concerned. (Tr.)

thus the naval command post which became the nerve-center of the defence. I must add that there were also a number of German units in Tobruk; but their C.O., General Diendl, was billeted about thirty miles away outside the perimeter and heard nothing of the attack until the following morning.

The first warning to reach Captain D'Aloja was a report that a British submarine had been sighted off the port very close inshore. Enemy submarines were in the Tobruk area almost every day, but not normally so close in. It seemed likely, therefore, that this submarine had some particular reason for penetrating so far into an area which was off the regular route for our own shipping. D'Aloja sent such anti-submarine craft as he had into action; but, being rather a job lot, they failed either to sink the submarine or get rid of her. They could only harass her, though to such good effect that she presently moved off further north. She moved, in fact, so far that she was unable to carry out her intended role of guiding in the British landing craft. She signalled them a position, it is true, but it was the wrong one, with the result that the marines later put ashore by the destroyers *Sikh* and *Zulu* found themselves a long way from their objective.

The presence of this submarine, then, gave the first alarm at Fortress H.Q. It was confirmed at about 2100 hours when an air attack began in quite unusual strength. It continued at the same intensity until 0300 hours. Meanwhile all our guards and picquets had been alerted. D'Aloja, still preoccupied with the submarine, also turned out the motor barges and stationed them along the boom defenses and off the more vulnerable beaches. No one else would have considered turning these transport boats into efficient instruments of war; but it turned out to be a happy thought, for they later put up a very good show.

Nothing further happened until midnight. It had begun to look as if an intruding submarine and a heavy air-attack were all that was intended, when the main attack developed and we

The Attack that Failed

began to see what the British were after. Just at midnight a report reached Naval H.Q. that units of the Long Range Desert Group, mounted on trucks, had penetrated the outer defenses from the landward side, made contact with commandos landed from assault boats at Mersa Shusc, south of Tobruk, and captured a 4-inch battery. So far the enemy's operations had gone according to plan. But when the LRDG and the Commandos attempted the next step—the capture of the naval 6-inch battery further south at Mersa Biad—things began to go awry, because the battery not only refused to be captured, but gave the general alarm to the fortress.

Lombardi, D'Aloja and Battaglia thus had a fairly clear picture of what was happening on the south side of the bay. The only troops available were one company of the San Marco naval battalion—120 seamen under Lt. Colotto—which they sent at once to Mersa Shusc. Other units of the San Marco battalion were already posted along the coast and came into action (very successfully) where they were. But there was no other reserve on which H.Q. could draw.

Apart from the LRDG and the Commandos, the British plan also provided for *Sikh* and *Zulu* to land about 400 marines on the north side of the bay at approximately 0100 hours. This was the landing point which the submarine should have marked. So it did, but none too well, since our anti-submarine craft had driven the intruder at least three miles north of his intended position. Consequently, when the landing parties from *Sikh* and *Zulu* got ashore, they found themselves in the middle of the desert instead of on the outskirts of Tobruk. Moreover, they bumped into an outpost—the one known to us as Fort Perrone—which gave the alarm, so that H.Q. were now informed of both prongs of the attack. But when they looked round for some troops with which to meet the threat from the north, they were forced to realize that, now the San Marco company had gone, there were none left. They took the appropriate action;

that is to say, they collected cooks, storemen, orderlies and headquarters clerks, German or Italian, added a few *carabinieri* and bundled them off to the threatened point. This incongruous team included forty seamen, forty *carabinieri* and thirty German soldiers, who had reported for duty of their own accord. On the way, the party was joined by another fifty *carabinieri* under the commander of the 18th CC. RR. Battalion. To the north, then, went 160 men collected at random; to the south the 120 seamen of the San Marco battalion. Nothing was left at H.Q., where a local defense had been organized in case the attack should penetrate right into the town, except sixty seamen and twenty-five men of the Italian African Police.

The order of battle of the defense was not imposing—very much the reverse. Yet it was those 160 cooks, orderlies, etc., who held the position in the north against the 400 marines from *Sikh* and *Zulu*; and Colotto's 120 seamen who pinned down the Commandos and the LRDG to the south of the naval 6-inch battery, and so enabled the battery to open a well-directed fire on *Sikh* and *Zulu* as they were withdrawing at dawn. Both ships were sunk.[1] A notable part was also played by the quick-firing batteries on the south side of the bay and the 4-inch Dandalo battery, another naval post, which was not yet operational but managed to bring two guns into action with crews drawn from the artificers who were mounting the battery. The cruiser *Coventry*, supporting the operation from a distance, was sunk by German and Italian aircraft.

But the real high spot of the defense—one might even call it a masterpiece—was the behavior of D'Aloja's motor barges when a group of British MTB tried to force the boom defenses. The barges were awkward boats to handle—perfect clowns in

---

[1] The boats landing her marines not having returned, *Sikh* moved inshore in search of them and was disabled by gunfire at 5:30 a.m. *Zulu*, having attempted unsuccessfully to tow her off, rejoined the supporting force; later she and the AA cruiser *Coventry* were both sunk by air attack. (Tr.)

The Attack that Failed

the water—but, armed with light cannon and a few machine guns, they turned themselves into formidable opponents, spouting fire like the Roman candles of our youth. The enemy found barges at Mersa Shusc and off all the beaches where they tried to land. Had they gone further, they would also have found them alongside all the wharves in the harbor. But the largest concentration was along the boom defenses, where between 0100 hours and 0600 hours a series of hand-to-hand battles developed between the barges and the enemy MTB. The barges maneuvred with the precision and hitting power of torpedo boats, despite the air attack which continued throughout the night, the confused position on shore and at sea and the difficulty of maintaining any central control.

Before striking a final balance, I must add that Admiral Lombardi, as soon as he became aware that a major attack was developing, sent off dispatch riders—the telephone lines had been cut—to General Diendl and to the Italian command under which Tobruk came, with requests for support. Diendl arrived in person at ten o'clock the following morning, but only to kick up a frightful row because we had had the impertinence to defeat the British without waiting for him. G.H.Q. dispatched some *Bersaglieri* contingents from Bardia, but these arrived too late to join in the fun. We did, however, receive one reinforcement in the shape of Admiral Girosi and General Ferrari, who jumped into a truck as soon as they heard the news and drove straight for Tobruk with an escort of two *carabinieri* armed with tommy guns, with the idea of acting as a liaison with G.H.Q. or, at any rate, joining the party themselves. I must also award an honorable mention to Signalman Zinni, who found the British operation order with its details of all the nice (or nasty) things that were going to happen at Tobruk and further down the coast. In fact they did not happen, partly as the result of a spirited local resistance and partly, I think, because the knowledge gained from the captured plan enabled the defense to deploy its limited resources where they were most needed.

The final balance sheet ran as follows: destroyers *Sikh* and *Zulu* sunk by the Tobruk batteries; cruiser *Coventry* sunk by air attack; at least six MTB and many landing-craft destroyed by motor-barges; *MTB 314* captured intact; over 600 prisoners, including the force commander. Italian losses: about 50 men all told.

XII

The *Kasbah*

Feltrinelli exchanged a few words, perhaps a password, with the old man and then followed him towards the outskirts of Alexandria. The old man was small and skinny, with a grey walrus moustache; his linen suit and panama were shabby and yellowish. The two walked on in silence until they reached the door of an isolated villa, hidden away among palms and casuarinas.

For Feltrinelli this was the prelude to a month of complete unreality, a grotesque film-script made up of scraps of Graham Greene, Robert Hichens and Buchan. It was the spring of 1942. He spent his month in the heart of an enemy city under the eyes of the police, not lurking, but living high, wide and handsome.

Luigi Feltrinelli was an attractive chap, fair, well-made, athletic and a bit of a cynic. He spent his war as the pilot of an assault boat, carrying out the most reckless and daredevil operations, only to die after the Armistice in a tragic but quite ordinary accident. I knew him first in Massawa in 1939, when he was combining the duties of engineer on the *Nullo* with the less austere but equally strenuous job—when you consider the climate—of captain of the destroyer's football team. We met again in Leros in December 1941, when the Alexandria operation was being planned.[1] He and the other pilots were our guests on the island while the submarine *Sciré* was stationed there before her successful mission. Feltrinelli took part in that operation as a supernumerary, his only job being to lend a hand when the others pushed off from *Sciré* and headed towards the enemy base. But in the repeat operation of May 1942 he had an active part, which finally led to his extraordinary adventures in the *Kasbah*.

Once more I will skip the operational details, in particular details of the improved defense which the British had organized after our coup of the previous December. It is enough to say that in May 1942 things went less smoothly. Some trick of the current carried the submarine *Ambra*, under Arillo's command, off her course and hampered what was a very delicate operation. As a result none of the three human-torpedoes was able to penetrate the harbor, not even the one piloted by Feltrinelli with the diver Favale as his number two. The pair coasted for some hours along the low-lying, marshy shore of Alexandria looking for some point of entry to the Naval Base. But in the end, under fire and shaken by under-water explosions, they decided that there was no hope of reaching their objective. They destroyed their *pig*[2] and landed about 3 a.m. right in the middle of the dockyard.

Feltrinelli decided not to give himself up, but to play possum instead in the hope of gaining time and perhaps organizing an escape back to Italy. He took off his diving-suit, sank it and removed the rank-badges from his overalls. (Pilots always wore their uniform under their diving-dress so that, if captured, they could claim the status of P.O.W.s.) He hoped that his clothes, which were shabby enough, might enable him to pass

---

[1] On 18 Dec. 1941, three Italian "human-torpedoes" penetrated the defenses of Alexandria and fixed delayed-action mines to the hulls of the *Queen Elizabeth* and the *Valiant*; both ships were seriously damaged.

[2] Nickname for human-torpedoes.

as a dockyard hand. He acted this part when he saw that the night shift was ending and joined the stream of workmen who were drifting sleepily towards the dockyard gates. A casual nod to the sentry and he was through and at large in Alexandria.

Our Secret Service was never as good as the British; but after two years of war it had managed to set up a certain organization, especially in Middle Eastern ports, which were always full of Italians. The rendezvous in Alexandria was in the park, where one could usually be certain of picking up a contact, if the occasion warranted it. It was there that Feltrinelli entered his unreal world.

The isolated villa to which he was taken contained a woman, a gorgeous blonde, who in the best film tradition fell in love with him, supplied him with clothes and money and found him a hideout in the *Kasbah*. There he lived for rather more than a month in an extraordinary cosmopolitan world of spies, thieves and black-marketeers.

If this had been all, it would have been odd enough though nothing out of the way, for thousands of people at one time or another must have hidden in the *Kasbah*. But Feltrinelli's story had an added twist. The blonde had no intention of keeping her protégé tucked away in the Arab quarter. She wanted him by her side, moving in the same circles as she did—that is to say, the best society in Alexandria, the most exclusive clubs and all the grandest parties. Feltrinelli had to embark on a double, or, rather, treble life, dividing his time between the villa, the *Kasbah* and the café society of Alexandria. He played his part to perfection. He made friends, squired old ladies, played bridge à la Culbertson at the best tables, drank the King's health at semi-official dinners and sat puffing Egyptian cigarettes and telling smoking room stories after the ladies had withdrawn. He heard the confidences of the most tightly-buttoned of high officials; he allowed certain elegant fingers to ruffle his hair; and, at intervals, he drank thick coffee with Levantines bartering sacks of rice for rubber balls or selling cotton for piastres, dollars, sterling or rupees.

But all good things must have an end. One day the police surrounded the *Kasbah*. It was said that they were searching for an Italian officer. Feltrinelli saw that the game was up, put on his overalls again with the rank-badges restored, and surrendered to the N.C.O. in charge of the picquet. He spent the rest of the war in a P.O.W. camp.

XIII

Villa Carmela

THE Villa Carmela—"Italy's most advanced naval base in enemy waters," as Valerio Borghese called it[1]—has been so often filmed and written about that the subject may well seem exhausted. Yet it is still worth while to say something more, if only to put the story back into its proper perspective. I should like to get rid of the thriller-writing and romance and come back to the facts, the real story of how this little white villa, hidden among the greenery of Puente Majorga, was converted into an offensive base only half a mile away from the British shipping in Gibraltar harbor.

Of course, there was a great deal of romance. Imagine a typical Spanish villa housing a newly-married couple. The husband is Antonio Ramognino, an Italian, apparently of no occupation other than fishing. His wife is the shy, retiring Conchita, who is recuperating in the Straits because her nerves have suffered in wartime Italy. The Governor of Algeciras is an occasional visitor at the villa; and outside, as often as not, stands the mysterious, though easily identifiable, "Mr. Perrera." And from the villa Italian frogmen secretly emerge to plant mines on British merchant ships.

Where could you find a better background for a thriller? It was so good that journalists and script-writers have felt bound

[1] In his book *Decima Flottiglia Mas*.

to add just that little more which makes the whole thing fantastic. But that was not a mistake which the actual organizers could afford to make. In fact, the whole operation was worked out with the same painstaking logic as a mathematical theorem; and the romantic accounts of the journalists—among which I include the article by a French admiral in *Hommes et Mondes*—have left out the best part of the story. How did the swimmers get to the Villa Carmela? And how was the villa stocked with all the requirements of a self-supporting base—diving-suits, aqualungs, explosives, limpet mines and all the rest?

Borghese, it is true, gives some account of this in his book; but he has left himself no space to linger over the details. He omits the episode, for instance, of Ramognino's arrest when his passport was out of order. Not that the passport mattered very much in itself; but it would have been awkward if the police had found the heavy automatic hidden in his Peugeot runabout....

To start at the beginning: Antonio Ramognino, who came from Genoa, was more than a newly-wed and apparently idle husband with no thought except for his wife's health. He was also the originator and chief of the whole project, so that a Spanish police enquiry, however it started, might well have had disastrous results. It would have meant the internment of Antonio and Conchita, the closing down of Villa Carmela and a sad end to a promising operation. However, he was able to get out of it that time by giving the name of Conchita's uncle, a high official in Madrid. After a couple of telephone calls, nothing happened but a small fine for having his papers out of order. No one, thank heaven, noticed the pistol.

But the real story starts rather earlier, on the day when Ramognino first submitted designs to the Admiralty for a new naval weapon. There is no need to describe his early plans and calculations or the process by which an instrument of war was converted into a project bristling with official stamps, seals and

Villa Carmela

serial numbers. The file went the usual rounds from one office or department to another, from Genoa to Spezia, from Spezia to Rome, from Rome to Levanto, until one day it landed in the hands of Moccagatta, who was then commanding the 10th Flotilla MAS.[1] He saw the importance of the invention at once, but was too busy planning his bold but ill-fated operation against Malta to be able to do anything about it. He wrote to Ramognino from Augusta, where his headquarters then were, saying that he would go further into the matter as soon as he got back to Spezia.

This was, in fact, one of the last letters that Moccagatta wrote, for he was killed by machinegun fire from an aircraft during the attack on Malta. I mention it only to show another facet of this remarkable man, who could find time to give serious thought to a new weapon, while planning a most difficult operation.

Moccagatta's death was a severe setback to Ramognino. In the summer of 1941, experiments were carried out on the beach at Levanto, though it was not until September that a meeting at Spezia between Ramognino, Borghese and Todaro set the project on the right path. Or nearly the right path because, in fact, that particular invention was never used against the enemy; but the contact with Borghese and a further inspiration by Ramognino led to the Admiralty decision to rent a villa on Spanish soil near Algeciras and use it as a base for undercover operations.

Borghese, who knew from experience how difficult and dangerous it was to launch frogmen or human torpedoes from a submarine on the surface of the Straits, gave the plan his warmest approval. He enlisted Ramognino, who was graded as unfit for service, as a volunteer in the 10th Flotilla and sent him and his wife off to Spain to look for a villa.

Antonio and Conchita entered Spain on 6 April 1942 in a

[1] Motor assault boats. (Tr.)

blaze of publicity. They travelled round the country in a car conspicuously labelled "Italian Mission," stopping at hotels where their arrival was always heralded in advance. But they managed to carry out their mission all the same with the invaluable help of a certain Doctor Falasco, who had previously lived in Algeciras, but had moved at the outbreak of war to a villa about five miles away.

We shall meet Falasco again. For the moment let us follow Antonio and Conchita, who found and rented near Puente Mayorga just the little villa which Conchita's health seemed to require. They also interested themselves in the Italian ships which were being repaired in Algeciras or were lying half-submerged in the harbor, where they had been sunk at the outbreak of war. There were three or four of them, including the *Lavoro*, the *Pagao* and the *Olterra*. It occurred to Ramognino that one of these, suitably equipped, would add to the base which he was planning to set up at the villa. Under cover of repair work, she could be fitted out with all the apparatus necessary for preparing and launching the complicated assault craft known officially as SLC's or slow torpedoes, but popularly called *pigs*. This was work which could not possibly be done at the villa.

The Ramogninos returned to Spezia, where Borghese at once approved the plan to set up not one but two operational bases within range of Gibraltar: the first on the tanker *Olterra* for the human torpedoes; the second at Villa Carmela for the frogmen.

Much has already been written about the *Olterra* and her crew—the famous *Ursa Major* team—and I shall have something to say myself in a later chapter about *Olterra's* commander, Lt. Licio Visintini, who sacrificed himself in Gibraltar harbor. But now we must concentrate on the Villa Carmela, which, though part of the same organization, formed a separate unit on its own. The villa opened for business at the beginning of

June 1942, as soon as the honeymoon couple were installed.

"We ordered a lot of furniture," writes Ramognino, "much more than was needed. We got it a little at a time from widely separated places and it was delivered in trucks which used to make long stops at Falasco's house on their way."

Falasco's house, you will remember, was out in the country and, since it stood inland, less exposed to the prying eyes of watchers like Mr. Perrera, who were permanently stationed all around the bay from La Linea to Algeciras. Accordingly, the furniture vans were diverted via Falasco's house, where their loads were completed.

"Our various bits of equipment—respirators, rubber suits, oxygen bottles etc.—reached us hidden inside the furniture. Two large bottles of compressed air, which were too big to travel this way, were dressed up in hats and coats and brought home at night on the back seat of the Peugeot. They looked like two half-asleep or drunken persons and fortunately nobody was sufficiently inquisitive to ask who they were. The problem of bringing in the limpet-mines was more serious. They could hardly go in the furniture and for some time we could not think of any way of fetching them from Falasco's. Finally, we solved the problem by hiding them in sacks of coal, which we ordered, of course, through Falasco. It was, perhaps, rather a large quantity for a small villa with only two people in it; but no one bothered to investigate."

The varied equipment was assembled at the villa; and this was not so easy as it may sound. It was essential, for one thing, to avoid arousing the suspicions of the Spanish part-time maid and not to leave about any identifiable trash, such as boxes, wax paper, rubber bags, empty bottles or unused explosives.

"We threw everything down the well behind the house at night, when no one could see us. It was a deep, unused well. After the operation on the night of 12 July, I also threw down some limpets which had not been used. They exploded about a couple of months later; but everyone thought it was a bomb dropped from an aircraft aiming at Gibraltar.

"The operation on the 12th was the first to start from the villa. That day there was a *fiesta* at La Linea, which drew a crowd of people from neighboring villages. We decided to take advantage of this to bring across to the villa the swimmers who had meanwhile arrived on *Olterra*. That evening, Conchita and I went to La Linea and danced where everyone could see us. Then we came home to get the operation ready . . . I had decided to take part myself, but received orders from Falasco to stay behind, as he considered my presence on shore more necessary."

In this operation—Borghese puts it on the night of the 13th not the 12th—twelve frogmen took part: two officers, two petty officers, two divers and six seamen. They left the villa after dark and made their way along the dry bed of a stream, whose wooded banks gave them cover for the few yards to the sea. They were, in fact, unobserved except by some dogs who started barking—fairly enough considering what was going on under their noses. But all was well; no alarm was given to whoever was watching the Villa Carmela. The twelve frogmen had a clear road to their objective, the merchantmen of a large convoy which was then in Gibraltar harbor.

That night the S.S. *Shuma, Baron Douglas, Meta* and *Empire Snipe* all blew up. That they were not all a total loss was only due to the speed with which the British managed to beach them. All four ships were put out of action for the duration. In fact, a total of ten ships had been mined; but the premature explosion of one limpet gave the alarm and the waters of the harbor were searched, the ships minutely examined and many of the charges removed. But not all. . . .

After this operation, all our men got back safely to Spain. Some reached the Villa Carmela; others were arrested on the

Villa Carmela

beach by *carabineros*, but released after the intervention of the Italian consul in Algeciras.

The odd thing is that the British did not realize at the time that the attack originated in Spain. They thought that the saboteurs had been dispatched from a submarine in the harbor as had happened a few months before at Alexandria and in the previous year at Gibraltar itself. Their destroyers and corvettes put out to sea at once to search for this suspected boat. But in the end they must have known or guessed the truth, because a triple barbed wire fence, decorated with chevaux-de-frise and other obstacles, was run out along the foreshore between Gibraltar and Algeciras. Mr. Perrera and his minions also began to bivouac permanently round the Villa Carmela—presumably not with the idea of serenading Conchita.

But it needed more than barbed wire or troops of Perreras to stop the villa. On the night of 15 September the frogmen were in action again. Only three ships were at anchor outside the naval basin and three swimmers accordingly went out: Lt. Straulino and Petty Officers Di Lorenzo and Giari.

"Everything was organized as before, but we had one new and unforeseen difficulty to overcome. Mr. Perrera was still on watch; but it had nothing to do with him. It took the form of an unexpected visit from General Molino, the Governor of Algeciras, his brother, who commanded the Naval Base, and their wives. I never discovered whether the visit was simply an unusual example of Spanish courtesy or whether some particular motive lay behind it. However, there they were. They arrived at the villa during the afternoon and stayed until late in the evening, while we were expecting the swimmers and had a thousand and one things to see to. And the house, as you can suppose, was upside down...."

I can imagine the scene. The frogmen's limpets in one corner; diving suits and aqualungs piled here and there; waterproof cases and bottles of oxygen all over the place; a forgotten box in the most conspicuous position; and, in the middle of the mêlée, Conchita giving her guests tea and chatting brightly about her uncle in Madrid. All this for hours, while everyone was waiting for Straulino, Di Lorenzo and Giari to arrive, as, in fact, they did a quarter of an hour after the guests had left at nine o'clock.

This time the operation was less successful, as only one ship, *Raven's Point*, was sunk. But by September the British had taken to berthing their ships directly opposite the naval basin, if not inside it, and to posting lookouts on board, who periodically threw explosive charges into the water. Consequently, to sink even one ship out of the three present was not bad work, especially when you remember that only three swimmers were employed, all of whom returned safely.

So ended the story of the Villa Carmela, a less romantic story than some people have made out, but for that very reason better worth the telling.

Makeshift landing-craft used in invasion of Crete.

A convoy at Gibraltar. Villa Carmela in left center.

Vivaldi *runs into heavy weather while on convoy duty.*

"Ghost" ship, the light cruiser Bartholomeo Colleo

nte Gargano *sinks after being hit by aerial torpedo.*

German steamer Castellon *succumbs to torpedo attack.*

Convoy about to sail from Italian base in Adriatic.

Typical Italian convoy en route to North A

XIV

The Ghost Ships

MUCH HAS been written, both in England and Italy, about the Battle of Cape Matapan. We know every last detail of that unhappy affair. We know the circumstances which led to the disastrous night-action; the courses of all the ships engaged; the positions of the British battleships and cruisers; the speed of the enemy destroyers which chased the damaged *Vittorio Veneto*, but failed to catch her; the movements of Admiral Cattaneo's cruisers, *Zara* and *Fiume*, which were both lost; and how it was that *Pola* came to find itself torpedoed and stationary in mid-ocean. In short, we know everything, both from Admiral Iachino's account and from the detailed analysis of the battle in Admiral Bernotti's history of the war. There would be no point in saying anything more, were it not for certain well-authenticated phenomena which occurred during the battle and of which mere commonsense can provide no explanation.

Not long ago, for example, a bottle was washed ashore containing a dying message from one of the enlisted men killed in the action off Matapan. The bottle was found on a beach in Sardinia. Inside was a paper bearing the words: "Signori, tell my Mother I am dying for my country. Thank you, signori, thank you." The writer was Francesco Chirico, a seaman from Futani; and his message was scribbled as his ship, the *Fiume*, was sinking. At the last moment he thought of something else and added after his name the words, "Italia, Italia." They expressed all that he felt, but did not know how to say, as his ship went down. He committed his message to the sea, and the sea faithfully delivered it eleven years later.

I have no wish to comment on this message from eternity. You will say that it was pure chance that a jettisoned bottle, adrift in the Mediterranean for eleven years, should find its way at last to an Italian beach. So it was. But it was a chance which fits exactly into the pattern of strange events surrounding Mapan. Some people may be able to find a prosaic explanation; but I cannot.

A great many things about the battle can be explained. We know, for example, why the British did not open fire at once after spotting the *Pola* by radar, but turned away in search of other ships, which might not have been there at all. We can understand how the course of our two cruisers came to coincide with that of the British 15-inch battleships and why it was that the British, well served by the planes from their aircraft carrier, knew exactly which Italian ships were at sea, whereas we had only a general idea that Cunningham's battle fleet was out. All this, as I say, can be explained. What remains entirely inexplicable is why seamen on both sides—the British without exception and many Italians as well—saw during the action a light cruiser of the *Colleoni* class, which was not in fact there at all.

There is no need to give an account of the whole engagement. It is enough to recall that on the night of 28 March, the cruiser *Palo*, badly hit by an air torpedo, was stationary, and that the heavy cruisers *Zara* and *Fiume*, with four destroyers under Admiral Cattaneo, had been sent to her aid. The cruisers were steaming in line ahead, *Zara* leading, followed by the destroyers. They were the only Italian ships moving in the area. *Pola*, though not far off, being still stationary. Yet all the British accounts maintain that ahead of *Zara*, the flagship, was a light cruiser of the *Colleoni* class. It was so reported at the time; and

Admiral Cunningham has told the same story in his recent memoirs. There is thus no room for doubt that the British officers and men concerned did actually see this non-existent ship.

The precise time at which she was first picked up is given: 2228 hours. She was a light cruiser of the *Colleoni* class and was sailing ahead of *Zara*, like an outrider to the Italian formation. It is also stated that she was fired on and that fires were started on board, which forced her to break off the action.

Zara and *Fiume*, as we know, not being equipped with radar, were taken by surprise and were both sunk before they could fire a shot. *Pola*, a silent and inactive spectator of the fight, was also sunk. But what of the light cruiser? No ship of that class took part in the engagement at any stage, either that night off Cape Matapan or earlier in the day off Gavdo Island. Her appearance was a myth or the result of mass-hallucination. But can any illusion of that sort be strong enough to persuade a captain and his crew to open fire on a ship which isn't there; or an admiral to report afterwards that the ship in question caught fire?

If it was an illusion, it was a strange one; and it is made all the stranger by the fact that, eight months before, the *Bartolomeo Colleoni* herself had been sunk in those very waters by the Australian cruiser *Sydney*. The *Colleoni* can scarcely have been actually present at Matapan; but her ghost was certainly there, drawing the enemy's fire. The enemy saw her, and she was also seen from the deck of the helpless *Pola*. But no one could do much for the Italian ships that night, not even a visible but non-existent light cruiser.

But the strangest story which that sad night action produced, is another. Admiral Iachino mentions it in his *Gaudo e Matapan* and so do other writers. I was told it by a seaman from Naples who was with me in the Red Sea and in the Atlantic in *Torelli* and was afterwards posted to *Fiume*. All that I can remember about him is that his name was Antonio. When he came to see me on *Da Recco*, he told me, with tears in his eyes, the story of *Fiume's* loss. The first salvo had taken her by surprise. Her Captain, Giorgio Giorgis, had tried in vain to bring the resulting fires under control, and had finally given the order to abandon ship. He himself had stayed on board; and they had seen him in the stern lighting a cigarette as he made his way forward to the bridge for the last time.

The survivors were adrift on rafts and in boats for five days. They suffered a good deal; but it was not that which left its mark on Antonio, so much as a sight which they all saw at dawn on the second day.

"There was nothing in sight, only flat, oily sea. So we all saw her plain enough when she began to come up, four or five miles away. First the crow's nest, then the mast and funnels. We couldn't help but know her. It was our own ship, *Fiume*, coming back for us. We could see her bridge and her gun turrets. She heaved herself out of the water till her decks were almost awash, but so slowly that we thought she was dying. We thought she had come to fetch us, because some of us were pretty far gone by then. But she stayed where she was without ever seeming to shake quite free of the water. Then, very slowly, she began to sink again and that was that."

That was the story that Antonio told me more than a year later. Perhaps I ought to have spoken to him about mirages and the power of suggestion. But who was I to destroy his belief that his ship had made a dying effort to rescue her crew? Besides, I am still convinced that *Fiume* did come back with a message for those who would listen, the same message that she sent last year by the hand of Francesco Chirico of Futani.

Part 3. CONVOYS

XV

The Battle of African Convoys

I

DURING the peace years, especially after the end of the Ethiopian War, the Italian Navy's General Staff made a detailed study of the problem of supplying an army operating in Lybia. Every phase was carefully considered. Finally, in 1938, a concrete operational plan was formulated. The studies and the final plan indicated that should Italy be involved in a war against both France and England that the logistical support of troops in Lybia would undoubtedly entail a great sacrifice of both men and ships and that its achievement would probably be impossible. Moreover, the plan of 1938 indicated the necessity for escorting our convoys in the central Mediterranean, if they were to arrive safely at their ports of debarkation, with all available warships and aircraft.

The General Staff was convinced that the Lybian sea routes would be intensively and constantly patrolled not only by the major British warships based at Gibraltar and Alexandria, but also by lighter vessels, submarines and aircraft concentrated at Malta. Considering the inferiority of Italian forces and their limited air and sea power compared to that of the enemy, a pessimistic outlook was by no means unjustified.

Among the various threats, Malta's offensive potentiality appeared particularly dangerous. The island, located in the middle of the sea lanes between Lybia and Italy, enabled ships and planes based there to attack our convoys at sea at short notice. In this respect, the above-mentioned plan of the General Staff reads as follows: "Initially, only a small force will be stationed on Malta . . . the strengthening of forces at Malta and Bizerte might actually make it impossible to transport troops and supplies to North Africa." The same study, passing from a general consideration to an evaluation of details, added: "We do not have at our disposal, at present, an aerial strength capable of escorting and protecting our convoys. The problem would be solved by the capture of Malta, for the other enemy bases, because of their remote distance, would not be capable of persistent aerial action against our convoys."

For various reasons, the occupation of Malta was not considered at that time. Consequently, on the eve of the war, the danger which that island presented to our Lybia-bound traffic was still present in all its acuteness.

The Italian geo-strategic situation was, on the whole, of such gravity as to persuade Admiral Cavagnari, Italian CNO, to write in a memorandum to the Chief of the General Staff on 6 April 1940: "Whatever character the war may assume in the Mediterranean the toll of our naval losses will, in the end, be very heavy. Italy might well arrive at the peace table not only with no territorial assets but also without a fleet and, perhaps, without an air force."

Admiral Cavagnari's thinking, of course, referred to our naval warfare in its entirety. There is no doubt, however, that the defense of our traffic with Lybia constituted the most pressing aspect of the Italian naval war.

Another pessimistic forecast on the possibility of maintaining our traffic with the African ports is to be found in another important document, namely, in the minutes of the meeting held by the Chiefs of Staff on 5 June 1940 presided over by Marshal Badoglio. War had already been decided upon, in fact, it was on the point of breaking out. When the question of supplies to Lybia was brought up, Marshal Badoglio, after stating that he would make use of all available civilian planes—and they were very few—was only able to make the following proposal which is contained in the minutes of the meeting: "We know that with six submarine minelayers we can carry about 600 tons per trip besides, a little can be risked in ships which, sailing from Port Empedocle, could reach the African coast overnight. In this manner, we can *hope* to supply Lybia."

From these documents one must necessarily infer that the various Chiefs of Staff considered the supplying of Lybia practically impossible, except: 1. By means of a few civilian planes, capable of transporting about thirty men each; 2. By six submarines with a capacity of about 100 tons each (Actually they seldom carried more than 60 tons.) 3. By small cargo vessels, which every now and then might sail from Port Empedocle.

The problem of supplying Lybia was therefore considered difficult of solution; so difficult in fact that it should not even be tackled.

And, in fact, when on 10 June 1940, Italy opened hostilities against France and England, the first supplies to North Africa were sent by plane, by submarine minelayers, destroyers and by small fast motorboats, precisely as the Chief of the General Staff had predicted.

It was on 25 June that the first real convoy composed of the *Esperia* and the *Victoria* loaded with a few hundred men and a few thousand tons of supplies sailed from Naples. Fifteen days of war were sufficient to demonstrate: 1. That to supply an army in Lybia required far more than a few submarines and destroyers; 2. That the central Mediterranean was not so much "off limits" to Italian navigation as had been thought before the war.

The High Command, on whom fell the responsibility of war, realized that the "Battle of Lybian Convoys," even difficult, bitter and unpredictable as it was, had to be tackled and fought.

At the beginning of July, the ponderous machinery of organizing and defending the convoys bound for Lybia was set in motion; a machinery whose efficiency grew steadily with the passing months; a machinery that at times had to cope with unforeseen difficulties and which could never keep pace with the technical progress of the enemy; a machinery which occasionally did not yield perhaps its full output (e.g. in the fall of 1941); a machinery, however, that in 31 months of war was able to transfer to Lybia nearly 2,000,000 tons of supplies with a loss of 14 per cent and 200,000 men with only a loss of 8.3 per cent.

Later we shall supply other data to document the final results of the battle of convoys, but we must state at this point that the Lybian ports at Italy's disposal could hardly absorb more than two million tons of goods. Such a conclusion is derived from a careful, analytical survey of the periods during which those ports were in Italian hands and the number of working days in each port. We do not think it necessary to report here the painstaking (and certainly not pleasant) analysis which we conducted. We shall limit ourselves to pointing out the perfect balance between the amount of supplies transported and the total amount which could actually have been unloaded. Such a tally is clear evidence that the "Battle of Lybian Convoys" was, in fact, fought most satisfactorily by the Italian Navy.

II

Only 200 Italian and 15 German cargo ships (of more than 500 gross tons) were actually used on the sea routes to Lybia. These ships shuttled unceasingly between the two coasts of the

African Convoys

central Mediterranean for a total of 1,789 runs. The ships actually used were roughly no more than the number above mentioned. No more, for the simple reason that the total number of merchant ships (tankers included) capable of the difficult task of supplying our troops in Tripolitania and Cyrenaica did not exceed that number.

It is quite true that in 1940 Italy had 786 ships of a gross tonnage above 500 tons, but at the outbreak of the war, one-third of them (nearly 1,240,000 gross tons) were out of the Mediterranean and consequently lost before a single shot was fired. Political considerations had prevented the ships from being called home even when war had already been decided upon.

As we shall see, in a following chapter, some of our ships surprised in foreign ports by the outbreak of the war managed to reach French ports, occupied by the Germans. Some of them, notably the MV *Orseolo* later succeeded in sailing to Japan. This, however, did not bring the slightest relief to our traffic in the Mediterranean.

Consequently, at the outbreak of the war, Italy had at her disposal in the Mediterranean only 500 ships with a gross tonnage of two million tons. Some of these, however, due to their large size (e.g. *Rex, Conte Di Savoia, Saturnia*) were not suitable to war service. Others were not suitable because of their limited size, of their age and, above all, of their slow speeds. In time of war, no ship with a speed of less than ten knots should have been used in the Mediterranean. In practice, however, even ships with speeds of nine, eight, and seven knots were used. It would have been absurd to use ships which made less than seven knots. Furthermore, not every usable ship could be assigned to the Lybian traffic. Some were needed to insure communication with Greece, Albania and the Aegean ports—communication which, at a certain time, was even more pressing than that of the African coast. It was also necessary to insure traffic between the major Italian islands and the metropolitan ports.

To sum up, there remained only 200 Italian and 15 German ships for the Lybian traffic. Ships ranging from the *Esperia*, *Conte Rosso*, *Oceania* and *Neptunia* were unfortunately all sunk but only after having completed ten, twenty and thirty crossings of the Mediterranean. The *Esperia* was lost on her thirty-sixth crossing and the *Conte Rosso* on her seventeenth. The liner *Marco Polo* was withdrawn from service after having shuttled unharmed forty times between Italy and Lybia. The tankers *Giorgio*, *Proserpina* and *Rondine* ploughed the seas until the fall of Lybia. The large German steamers *Ankara*, *Reichenfels*, *Marburg*, the slow toilsome Italian *Gualdi*, *Nirvo* and *Agata*, the tiny German *Adana*, *Castellon* and *Alikante*, the indefatigable and precious Italian *Beppe*, *Ernesto*, *Nita*, *Maddalena* and *Nicolo Odero*, the *Achille Lauro*, the beautiful MV *Monginervo*, *Napoli*, *Pisani*, *Venier* and *Rialto*—all carried out several missions to Lybia before being sunk. The whole roster would be far too long and tedious to list. It suffices only to mention the various types of ships.

At the beginning of 1942, the first, fast cargo ships projected and built during the war began active service. It was mainly due to their constant activity that, in the spring of 1942, it was possible to assemble in North Africa the supplies, ammunition, arms, trucks and fuel, which enabled the triumphant offensive of Rommel's Italo-German troops to reach El Alamein.

From 10 June 1940 to 23 January 1943 (the fall of Tripoli), the Italian Navy staged a total of 896 convoys in the central Mediterranean supplying troops to Lybia. The number of runs has already been stated, 1,789 for a gross tonnage of 1,821,566 tons.

Since we have already given statistics, we may as well point out that on the sea routes to and from Lybia, we lost 151 mer-

African Convoys

chant ships for a total gross tonnage of 1,821,566.*

Incidentally, the British and Allied merchant fleets lost more than 20,000,000 tons during the war.

We shall soon speak at length of the causes for the loss of 151 ships and of the way the enemy carried on its offensive against our Lybian traffic. It is significant that these losses, based on the total number of runs, were limited to 8.4 per cent of the total gross tonnage employed.

To the convoys sent to Lybia are to be added another 378 organized for the bridgehead set up in Tunisia in the late fall of 1942 and held until the following spring. This amounted to an additional 1,279 runs for a total of 1,349,388 tons. Of these 224,345 were lost in enemy action—a percentage loss greater than that suffered on the Lybian routes. This is not at all surprising in view of the increasing intensity and efficiency of the enemy action as well as the contemporaneous shrinking of the war potential. The Italians received no help from the German Navy or the Luftwaffe.

As a matter of fact, in the naval struggle to supply our fighting troops, the Italian merchant fleet was practically totally destroyed. One-third was lost because of being in foreign ports at the outbreak of the war; 800,000 gross tons were lost in harbors as a result of air bombardments; 650,000 gross tons were sunk by enemy action on the routes to Lybia; and the rest was lost while navigating in home waters or on the routes to Greece, Albania, the Aegean, Sicily, Sardinia. During the last phase of the war, losses were suffered while trying to supply the Italo-German bridgehead in Tunisia.

---

* These figures refer only to merchant ships lost *at sea* on the Lybian routes. Total losses of Italian merchant shipping were in fact as follows:

Cause	Gross Tonnage
Sunk by submarines	810,093
Sunk in port by aircraft	378,058
Sunk at sea by aircraft	396,181
Sunk by surface ships	122,791
Sunk by mines or other causes	399,398
Interned abroad at outbreak of hostilities	1,240,000
	3,346,521

The war lasted thirty-one months in Lybia and four months in Tunisia and the accumulation of losses month after month could result only in the total destruction of our merchant fleet in three years.

One must marvel at the fact that early in 1943 we still had merchant ships able to sail the Tunisian route, a sea lane that Italian seamen rightly called the "death route."

III

It is not inappropriate that the term "battle" is used in speaking of the naval struggle to supply Lybia rather than another term which might seem more appropriate. As a matter of fact, the struggle consisted of one single battle which lasted thirty-one months or 930 uninterrupted days.

It was a single battle because of the restricted area in which it was fought. It was a battle with one purpose because the concept of operations were constant. It was one continuous battle because, as we shall see shortly, not a single day of those thirty-one months went by without an engagement around some convoy.

It was hand-to-hand struggle of maneuvers, of attacks and counter-attacks begun and decided in the space of a few minutes. Altogether, it was a war operation to be viewed, studied and evaluated in its entirety. The thousands of encounters that made up the Mediterranean adventure are bound together like the links of a single chain.

The "Battle of Lybian Convoys" lasted until the fall of Tripoli. Afterwards, the sea struggle shifted to another theater of operations and the battle to supply the Italo-German bridgehead established in Tunisia began. But the two operations must be considered separately, not only on account of the different areas in which they took place but also because the strategic situation was different in each one.

The "Battle of Lybian Convoys" lasted 930 days and almost 900 (896 to be exact) convoys sailed between Italy and Lybia.

It is apparent that the number of convoys nearly totalled the number of days of the battle. It is evident that practically every day of the war saw at least one convoy at sea between Italian Lybian ports. This does not mean that convoys left daily with the regularity and speed of express trains. For days and even weeks, none sailed. Other days, two, three or four sailed from Italian ports for Lybia or vice versa. It is in this manner that we arrive at the almost exact correlation between the number of convoys staged and the number of the days of the "battle." Since each crossing lasted several days—up to four for the slow convoys between Naples and Tripoli—it happened that not a single day of the war went by without at least one convoy being at sea between Sicily and Tripoli or between the Ionian and the north African coast. Every day there was at least one convoy, often several, straggling simultaneously along the routes headed north towards Italy or south towards Africa.

It was an uninterrupted battle, which in theory began 10 June 1940 but, in reality, began in December 1940 for it was in the latter month that the action and reaction assumed the continuity which was later to characterize the struggle until the end. In any case, it was a ceaseless struggle fought for thirty-one, or more accurately, twenty-five months.

During the course of the "battle" the overwhelming majority of the ships which sailed from port reached their destination safely, as may be seen by the statistical data already given. When we say safely we do not mean uneventful. As a matter of fact, the crossings of our convoys in the central Mediterranean were never uneventful. They were indeed extremely harassed, especially after December 1940. From that time on, there was not a single convoy that was not attacked—often several times —by airplanes, by British submarines, and sometimes (four or five times, and always at night) by surface ships which were usually extremely cautious in approaching the central Mediterranean.

In the course of such attacks some of our convoys were completely destroyed. Such was the fate of the *Tarigo* and *Duisburg* convoys. Several liners were lost to enemy submarine action, such the *Conte Rosso*, the *Oceania* and the *Neptune*. In the main, however, the battle put up by our escort units always ended quite satisfactorily for the Italians.

It would be wrong to draw conclusions only from the analysis of the few, particularly unfortunate experiences suffered by the Italian Navy. An exact evaluation of the results of the "Battle of Lybian Convoys" can only be obtained by considering the general picture of the "battle" and the statistical data which sum it up.

IV

The theater in which the "battle" took place—perhaps the longest battle in history—might be considered not much larger than a glass of water or, if you prefer, a handkerchief.

A mere glance at a map is enough to show how the Lybian convoys were squeezed by geography into a quadrilateral, limited on the north by the line which joins Cape Bon with the Strait of Otranto, and on the south by the coastline from Tripoli to Tobruk.

The supply routes to Lybia could only originate from ports of the Italian peninsula or from those of Sicily and could only terminate at Tripoli, Bengasi or Tobruk. No matter how much one might wish to alter ones courses or take long detours, the convoys were restricted to navigating inside the extremely limited quadrilateral, the boundaries of which we have just outlined.

When Tobruk was in British hands—and it was for eighteen out of the thirty-one months of the Lybian war—our convoys could only use the ports of Tripoli and Bengasi. When, because of enemy occupation or of being too encumbered with debris and exposed to enemy action, Bengasi could no longer be used, the only sea room available to convoys was reduced to a tri-

African Convoys

angle: a sort of funnel based on Tripoli toward which all merchant shipping bound for North Africa converged. Such was the situation throughout the winter of 1941.

The British knew that the Italian convoys were sorely restricted to a specific area which was completely cramped into this tight funnel. They soon realized that, except for rare periods, at least one convoy each day was at sea in these well-defined waters. They had a relatively easy time spotting, shadowing, then attacking every convoy at sea. As we mentioned earlier, the British had a most strategic base of operations at Malta right in

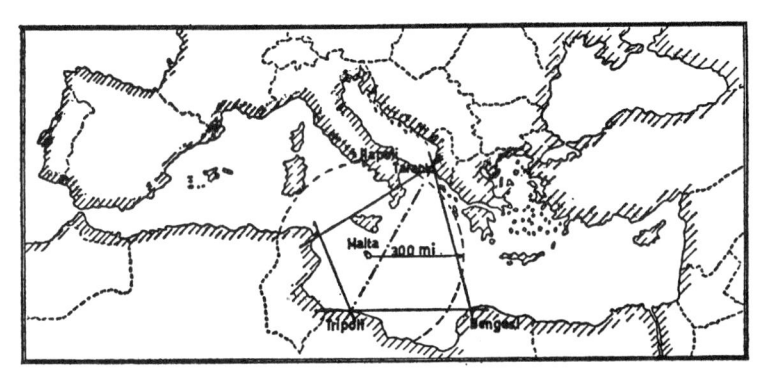

Italian convoys' areas of operation.

the middle of the theater in which the "battle" was taking place. Things became even easier for them when, in the summer of 1941, they could avail themselves of the radar-equipped planes for search and reconnaissance of our merchantmen.

A couple of such planes had only to fly over the quadrilateral or the triangle in which our convoys were restricted and the British knew immediately the location and the course of the convoy. It was then quite simple to alert the combat planes based on Malta, the submarines stationed in the area or (rarely) their surface ships based on Malta. It should be noted that the convoys proceeded at not more than ten knots and, frequently, even less.

Everything, in short, was on the enemy's side: the geographical situation, the strictly restricted fighting area, the offensive radar tactics and the slow speed of the majority of the convoys. And yet, in thirty-one months of war, we succeeded in transporting to Africa 1,929,955 tons of supplies (including fuel) and 189,162 men, with a loss of only 14% of the supplies and 8.3% of the men entrusted to the Navy.

We must produce more statistical data. This time, however, these are indispensable to an accurate understanding of the "Battle of Lybian Convoys." Merely for the sake of comparison, it must be pointed out that while the Italian merchantmen convoyed between Italy and Lybia totalled nearly 1800, the British ships which tried to cross the Mediterranean up until November 1942 totalled only about 100. These are grouped into twelve convoys. Most of these, if not all, were attacked and hampered by every possible means. Some were completely destroyed—like the convoy of March 1942. Others were forced to return to port—like the Alexandria convoy of June 1942. Another was almost entirely annihilated at Pantelleria. The convoy of August 1942 was literally obliterated by submarines, M.T.B.'s, airplanes, assault craft, predominantly Italian.*

* For the reader's convenience, the essential figures relating to the Lybian traffic are here summarized:

Convoys staged	896
Ships convoyed	1,789
Ships sunk	151
Percentage of losses related to the number of runs	7.2 per cent
Total tonnage convoyed	8,245,381 gross tons
Total tonnage lost at sea	642,677 gross tons
Percentage of losses	8.4 per cent
Materiel loaded	2,245,381 tons
Materiel arriving in ports	1,929,955 tons
Percentage of losses	14 per cent
Men embarked	206,402
Men reaching destination	189,162
Percentage of losses	8.35 per cent

V

Italian convoys in the Mediterranean were organized along quite different lines than were American or British convoys in the Atlantic and the Pacific. Allied convoys consisted of 40, 70, or even 100 merchant ships, escorted by scores of destroyers, corvettes, and aircraft carriers. Italian convoys, on the other hand, were much smaller. This restriction was imposed by the constricted sea room; by operational requirements, of which we shall speak later; and by the limited unloading capacities at the ports of destination. It is obvious that it would have been useless and dangerous to allow more ships to arrive at Tripoli, Bengasi or Tobruk than could simultaneously be unloaded. At Tripoli, for instance, no more than four or five ships could be unloaded simultaneously. When Bengasi was already overcrowded with three or four ships, it would have been absurd to allow a greater number to arrive there. These figures, by the way, represent the maximum unloading capacity of those ports and, consequently, dictated the maximum number of ships to be herded together in a single convoy headed for Tripoli or Bengasi. However, these ports did not enjoy this capacity at all times. For several months their capacity for absorption was far less. The reduction of the number of merchantmen that could arrive at the same time necessitated a reduction in the number of ships in the convoys.

Occasionally, under pressing requests from Army Commands, we tried to increase the rate of supply by speeding up the rhythm of convoys, disregarding the unloading facilities of the terminal ports. This measure at once proved to have such disastrous consequences that the Army ordered some of the unloaded ships back to sea. For example, this happened to a fine convoy of six merchantmen at Tripoli in 1941 under the escort of destroyers of the *Aviere* class. The harbor was so congested that the ships had to wait ten days for their turn. Finally, due to the possibility of air raids and to the imminent arrival of another convoy, the ships had to leave the harbor although they still had more than half of their cargoes aboard.

To make a long story short, it would have been absurd: 1. To stage convoys of more than five or six ships because no more could have been unloaded at a given time; 2. To allow a convoy of five to six merchantmen to arrive at a given port before the preceding convoy had been completely unloaded.

The number of ships in each convoy was therefore determined by the unloading capacity of the Lybian ports.

The limited logistic capabilities of Tripoli, Bengasi and Tobruk were repeatedly discussed by a committee of high-ranking generals and admirals attached to the Supreme Command which dealt with the problems of the Lybian traffic. Not even this authoritative body succeeded in boosting the unloading capacity of Bengasi's harbor to more than 500 to 600 tons a day, because this port was encumbered with wrecks of every description and battered piers. Besides, the town was bombed daily by Anglo-American planes. This same committee was unable to increase the working capabilities of Tobruk in the fall of 1942.

It was therefore impossible to increase the number of ships in each convoy. As the war went along, the numbers decreased because of the lessened capacity of the ports. Toward the end, each convoy consisted of only two or three ships. Also, the Italian Navy was compelled to reduce the number of ships in each convoy because of the lack of ships and because of the scarcity of raw materials at home. There is no doubt, however, that the principle reason is to be found in the exceedingly poor logistical capacity of the ports in North Africa.

VI

Obviously, the defense of the Lybian convoys could not be standardized. It had to be geared to the anticipated attacks along the sea routes.

We do not need to spend much time demonstrating that the kind of protection which was suitable against submarines and airplanes was valueless against cruisers or battleships or vice versa. Therefore, when speaking of convoy escorts, one must make a clear distinction between what was done to protect our ships from the attacks of surface ships and from that of submarines, bombers and torpedo planes.

Rarely did the threat from major British surface ships materialize. As a matter of fact, it was only in the summer of 1940 that it was deemed necessary to protect our convoys from the potential threat of the British fleet. Accordingly, in the first months, Italian shipping was often escorted by squadrons of cruisers and by the two battleships Italy had at the time, the two old, renovated *Ceasare* and *Cavour*, armed with 320 mm. guns.

At the beginning of July 1940, a convoy consisted of a few merchantmen, some headed for Bengasi and others for Tripoli, was escorted by the entire Italian fleet. The convoy reached its destination undamaged notwithstanding the presence in the vicinity of Malta of the entire British Mediterranean fleet consisting of three battleships armed with 381 mm. guns and an aircraft carrier bristling with torpedo planes. It was this convoy escort that precipitated the battle of Punta Stilo.

At that time our battleships—not only the remodernized ones but also the new 35,000-tonners as soon as they were ready early in August 1940—always protected our convoys whenever it was known that the enemy's battleships were at sea. In protecting our convoys, our battleships carried out a total of 15 missions and the cruisers 141, all of which were crowned with conspicuous success.

Until the end of December 1942, the Lybian convoys destroyed by British surface ships were the *Tarigo* and the *Duisberg* (consisting respectively of five and seven merchantmen), and the German convoys *Veloce* and *Maritza* (respectively of three and two ships). This means four convoys on routes to and from Lybia in thirty months of war. We shall examine the very special circumstances under which these were destroyed.

Let us begin with the *Tarigo* and *Duisberg* convoys. The first was attacked by four destroyers and the second by two light cruisers and two destroyers, both during the night, when radar, which the British had and we did not, endowed the enemy with an overwhelming and indisputable superiority. Such nocturnal actions at sea may be compared to a duel between a blind man and a man who enjoys perfect vision: unfortunately, we were the blind ones. The British soon realized the advantage of making use of radar at night. Especially after Matapan, whenever possible, they always resorted to night actions.

In order to attack the *Tarigo* and the *Duisburg* convoys, the British units sailed from Malta at sunset, thus gaining complete surprise. After detecting the convoys by radar, rather than attacking at once, they waited leisurely until they had attained a more advantageous position before sighting their guns and opening fire. Even in the British reports, it appears that the *Tarigo* and the *Duisburg* were kept under radar observation for twenty-one and seventeen minutes, respectively, before the attack was launched. These were very long minutes during which the British could see our ships while we did not have the slightest idea that they were at sea and, even less, that they were on the verge of attacking us. The British used these undisturbed long minutes to maneuver, to outdistance the escort and to surround the merchantmen.

When they open fire—and it was only then that their presence was revealed to our ships—they did so with dead sure odds, as their radar had already provided them with the exact bearings and range. The *Duisburg* was escorted by a squadron of 10,000-ton cruisers and ten destroyers. None of them were able to intervene successfully because of the manner in which the action was carried out. The seven merchantmen of the convoy were set afire in a few minutes. Two destroyers, the *Fulmine* and the *Libeccio* were lost.

The destruction of the *Tarigo* convoy, consisting of five small ships, most of them German, required slightly more time and cost the British the loss of the large destroyer *Mohawk* sunk by the *Tarigo*.

The loss of those two convoys and some of their escorts was a disheartening experience for the Italians and aroused justifiable and general commotion throughout Italy. These, however, were two, entirely sporadic incidents.

The *Veloce* convoy, consisting of three merchantmen, was also sunk at night by radar-equipped ships. On the other hand, the German *Maritza* and *Procida*, escorted by the torpedo boats *Lupo* and *Cassiopea*, were sunk during daylight by a squadron of cruisers. They were the only ships in the entire "Battle of Lybian Convoys" sunk by surface units in a day action and in this case the enemy forces were overwhelming superior to ours.

It is indeed remarkable that in only one engagement—and with a formidable superiority of forces—the surface units of our Mediterranean adversary managed to destroy but one modest Lybian convoy by daylight. On other occasions, the enemy attacked by night and practically in absolute safety. The balance of the offensive against the Lybian traffic was carried out by submarines and aircraft.

Between Italy and Lybia, we had established an almost uninterrupted stream of steamers, motorships and tankers which went back and forth day and night. Yet, the British fleet never thought of interfering with this continuous stream of ships except during the first months of the war. And still, the real objective of the naval war in the Mediterranean was right there, in the form of the Italian convoys travelling uninterruptedly between Italy and Lybia and supplying our army in North Africa.

We had all expected, and such was the general conviction,

that as soon as the war broke out, the British would hover in the middle of the Mediterranean with all their air and sea forces to sever all maritime links between Italy and Lybia. This they did not do, nor even attempted to do. It is therefore understandable why we considered it necessary, only on rare occasions, to escort our convoys with large dispositions of our fleet.

Had British strategy been dictated by the principle of attacking our sea communications with the whole strength of their fleet, the Mediterranean would undoubtedly have witnessed a series of major sea and air actions. British strategy chose, instead, to fight Italian traffic stealthily rather than with the fleet spread out in battle formation. Consequently, the Mediterranean was the stage for a series of duels between light units, submarines, and airplanes.

VII

When no attacks by British battleships and cruisers were expected, when their major units were known to be at anchor at their bases at both ends of the Mediterranean, when it was evident that our Lybian traffic could only expect attacks from submarines and day or night air raids, it would have been not only useless, but indeed dangerous, to entrust its protection to warships of substantial tonnage. Such units would have been helpless against submarines or airplanes. Because their size presented an easy target, they would have been exposed to serious hazards. This was particularly true when attacks took place at night, as was almost invariably the case from the end of 1941 on.

In this respect we must point out that the cruiser *Diaz* while on escort duty was sunk at night by an enemy submarine, and that the cruisers *Garibaldi, Bolzano, Trieste, Duca Degli Abruzzi* were also hit—but luckily not lost—by airplanes or submarines while escorting convoys. We must also remember that the battleship *Vittorio Veneto* was hit by a submarine's torpedo while escorting a convoy in December 1941.

It is clear that when the offense against the traffic was based on stealth, the corresponding defense had to be entrusted to naval and air units capable of frustrating the offensive means, that is to say, to light, torpedo craft equipped with electro-acoustic submarine detectors and to pursuit or anti-sub planes.

The number of light vessels assigned to each convoy was not fixed. It gradually grew with the progress of the war and with the increasing aggressiveness of British submarines. Thus, at the beginning of the war, we had convoys of three to four merchantmen escorted by two or even only one destroyer. In 1942 convoys of the same size had to be escorted by five, six or seven destroyers.

Generally, troop convoys were always provided with a heavier escort. It must be remembered, however, it was not always sufficient to encircle the transports with a strong ring of destroyers to insure their absolute safety. The *Oceania* convoy, consisting of three ships lost the two liners, *Oceania* and *Neptunia*, both sunk by submarine, although escorted by five destroyers. Conversely, in 1942 some rather lightly escorted convoys succeeded in eluding all submarine attacks. Obviously, luck played an important part in the game.

The convoys had the choice of passing east or west of Malta. Whatever course they chose, they had to travel the well-defined sea room which we have already mentioned. They were restricted to a sort of rigid rail leading to few, sometimes a single, port of call. This enormously facilitated the attackers plan of action.

Inevitably, some submarines were lurking off the ports of departure, or among the passages between the islands, or in the areas of arrival, or along the approaches to the Lybian coast. Often, the attacks were launched at night. It is useless to deny that nighttime was our weak spot during the entire war. It was after sunset, just off Messina Straits, that the *Conte Rosso* was torpedoed and sunk. She was part of a convoy of four liners escorted by numerous destroyers and a cruiser division.

It was again at night that the MV *Oceania* and the MV *Neptunia*, proceeding in a convoy with the *Vulcania* and escorted by five destroyers—all veterans of Lybian convoys—were torpedoed by submarines. They had followed a course east of Malta, keeping 160 miles away from the island to avoid torpedo bombers and they were about 70 miles from Tripoli when then ran into a group of three submarines. Of these, only the *Upholder* managed to gain a firing position and at 0410 18 September 1941 at a range of 4,000 meters, fired a salvo of torpedoes which hit and sank two targets, the MV *Neptunia* and the MV *Oceania*.

The *Vulcania* continued, escorted only by the *Usodimare*. About thirty miles from Tripoli, she was fired upon by another submarine. She successfully avoided being hit and reached port unharmed.

We are, of course, unable to list here all the ships which were torpedoed. The list would indeed be too long. We must limit ourselves to pointing out that, on the routes between Italy and Lybia, British submarines sank a total of 68 Italian and German ships amounting to approximately 302,000 gross tons.

The submarine was the weapon which inflicted the most serious losses to Italian merchant shipping. But this success came at a very high price. Great Britain lost 41 submarines in the Mediterranean; the French one and the Greeks three. All of them operated under orders of the British Admiralty.

Many other submarines were damaged by our destroyer escorts, but it is impossible to give the exact number.

VIII

British aerial offensive actions against our convoys began to be noticeable only in December 1940. In the beginning, the actions were timid, but aggressiveness gradually increased as the months went by.

The most effective defense against such an offense would have been our use of pursuit and combat planes. However, this was not always possible, because of organizational difficulties and, mainly, because of the shortage of planes.

For this reason, our convoys were at times escorted by a limited number of planes and for only a portion of their trip. On other occasions, there were no escort planes at all. The defense of convoys against air attacks had to depend entirely upon the anti-aircraft power of the escorts.

At night, neither the convoys nor the escorts had any aerial protection, for neither the German nor the Italian planes were properly equipped for night reconnaissance or combat. When the British realized this, they began to attack the convoys primarily at night. In fact, it may be said that from the fall of 1941 on, they attacked almost exclusively at night under conditions of practically absolute safety.

To detect our merchantmen, radar was generally used. Once the ships were located, they were illuminated by flares and deluged by bombs and torpedoes. The latter, it must be said, did not always reach their targets. Our ships could neither see nor hear the attackers, because they had neither radar nor escorting planes. Consequently, as soon as they were lit up by flares, they could only resort to the laying of smoke and to frequent changes of course in the hope of confusing the enemy. During the brief intervals in which the dim outlines of low-flying planes emerged from the darkness, the ships opened fire with all available machine guns.

Attacks which lasted three, four, or five hours or even the entire night put a severe strain on the morale of the crews, who had the feeling of being entirely at the mercy of the enemy. Every now and then, flames or a series of flares would light up the scene as in daylight. This would be followed by a shower of bombs and torpedo tracks. A lull might follow, but the crews knew that the enemy was still above them, waiting for a favorable opportunity—for a gap in the smokescreen or for the inevitable dispersal of the formation.

Anyone who sailed the Lybian routes in 1941 or 1942 will certainly not forget those nocternal sarabands of British airplanes and Italian ships, nor those thick smokescreens laid by the escorts as well as the convoy. These were the only means of defending the convoy against aerial attacks.

Night evasive maneuvers were sometimes successful and at other times caused considerable disorder in the formation. Maneuvering was possible only if the formations were simple and easy to handle and if the ships' captains were skilled in shiphandling and in quickly sizing-up the situation. This necessitated the reduction of the number of ships in each convoy to not more than three or four. Only formations of three or four merchant ships or, better still of two or three ships, were capable of maneuvering at night with the desired speed and the necessary quick turns. Not more than two ships could find their way through smokescreens or change course quickly enough when it was estimated that planes overhead were about to drop their bombs or torpedoes.

Because of the impossibility of countering the enemy's aerial offensive with opposing Italian or German fighters, we attempted to avoid the gravest danger—namely, the torpedo bombers—by keeping the convoy routes out of the range of the planes based on Malta. This proved easy enough as long as their range did not exceed 130 to 160 miles. It grew more difficult when their range began to reach 200 miles and, finally, impossible when their range reached 300 miles. From then on, all convoys were regularly mauled by torpedoes day and night.

To sum it up, 55 ships or 247,770 gross tons of Italian and German ships were sunk by bombers or torpedo bombers on the Lybian routes.

African Convoys

In the most critical periods of the "Battle of Lybian Convoys" Supermarina resorted to submarines and light naval craft for the rapid transporting of supplies, fuel, and men to Lybia. The cruisers *Barbiano* and *Giussano* and the submarines *Saint Bon*, *Caracciolo*, *Romolo*, *Atropo*, and *Remo* were all lost in enemy action while being used as transports. In 1941, submarines transported about 4,000 tons of gasoline and ammunition. Gasoline was also transported by the cruiser *Cadorna*. A squadron of destroyers ferried more than 10,000 men. In the summer of 1942, gasoline and ammunition were transported by the *Da Recco* and *Aviere* squadrons. Unfortunately, this was but a drop of water in the great sea of supplies needed by the fighting troops. The Navy, notwithstanding the ever-present enemy opposition, managed to carry this drop.

XVI

Blockade Runners

Anyone who had suggested before the war that Italian ships would be able to make successful voyages between France and Japan under the conditions prevailing from 1940 to 1943, would have been regarded as mad. In 1938 or 1939 no sane man would have predicted that Italy, while at war with both Great Britian and the United States, would still be able to allow herself the luxury of sending ordinary cargo-carrying ships halfway round the world, across the Atlantic, the Indian Ocean and the Pacific.

Nevertheless, it was done; and it was one of the most remarkable achievements of the war. The ships in question were unarmed merchantmen, sailing independently. They set out in the first place from neutral ports where their crews had been enjoying a comfort and security which many people might have envied. But when the call came, the hazards of which were obvious, they responded without hesitation. To do so needed courage of a particular kind—courage which for once was not measured in terms of the number of men killed. They weighed anchor and left their ports of refuge, loaded deep with merchandise and raw materials which were unobtainable in Axis Europe.

Three ships left from the Far East, the M.V. *Cortellazzo*, *Orseolo* and *Fusijama*. The first named sailed with 6,000 tons of cargo and an extra load of fuel in her bilge tanks. She left Korea on 16 November 1941, disguised as a Japanese, crossed the Pacific, rounded Cape Horn and sailed up the Atlantic to Bordeaux, where she arrived on 28 January 1942, seventy-two days out from Dairen, after a voyage of 21,000 miles. A chance encounter in the Pacific had forced her to make a sudden change of course; and Japan's entry into the war had involved a new disguise, improvized with some canvas and a few drums of paint. But these were her only difficulties.

Orseolo and *Fusijama* were equally successful. They left Kobe on 2 December 1941 and 7 February 1942, each with about 6,000 tons of useful cargo. *Fusijama's* voyage was the more eventful of the two. She was sighted several times by enemy ships, attacked by Japanese aircraft in the Pacific and intercepted by a British aircraft in the South Atlantic. But the Japs did no harm and the Englishman, evidently a decent fellow, was satisfied with her disguise. So *Fusijama* also got home safely.

We have seen already that thirty-six of the 220 Italian ships caught outside home waters at the outbreak of war were captured by the British. Another large group, mainly passenger ships, were interned by the United States, who returned nearly all of them at the end of the war—*Conte Grande, Conte Biancamano, Aida Lauro, Mar Glauco, Iole Fassio, Saturnia, Voluntas,* etc. Many others were able to take refuge in neutral ports or in Italian ports in the Red Sea. In 1941, these last found themselves in a very awkward position, hemmed in between the British bases at Suez and Aden and without any friendly or neutral port for which to run. There were thirty-seven of them in all, of which most were scuttled when Massawa and Assab fell to the British. *India, Sannio II, Piave* and some others were all lost in this way. The *Duca degli Abruzzi* and *Somalia*, on the other hand, were able to reach Diego Suarez, though they too were sunk in the end, when the British captured that port.

The M.V. *Himalaya* had a much happier fate. After a daring passage through the Perim Straits, she managed to escape the enemy's search and reached Brazil on 3 April 1941, after a voyage as bold as it was uneventful. She did not linger in Brazil but left again shortly with a cargo of hides and metal and arrived in Bordeaux on 30 April 1941.

Other ships from the Red Sea, including *Ramb I*, *Ramb II* and *Eritrea*, made for the Far East.[1] Both *Ramb II* and *Eritrea* reached eastern ports safely, though only after a number of unwelcome encounters, from which they escaped by skilful navigation and an adroit use of smoke. While crossing the Malay Archipelago, *Eritrea* (Commander Iannucci) had to take on Portuguese nationality—a disguise effected, as usual, by a lavish use of paint, some canvas, a little timber, and, of course, a Portuguese flag. The result was apparently good enough to deceive the Dutch aircraft, which circled her several times, trying to make out her identity. At any rate, they allowed her to pass.

Luck, on the other hand, ran against *Ramb I* (Commander Bonezzi) and led her straight into the arms of the cruiser *Leander* in the Indian Ocean. She tried the ruse of running up English colors but was ordered to heave-to. *Ramb I* then hoisted her own colors and opened fire with her two guns. The battle lasted about an hour; but gun duels between cruisers and merchantmen can only end one way.

The problem confronting our ships in South American ports was less difficult—though still far from easy—since they had no narrow waters to pass. But, in fact, only a few of them chose to face the risks of an Atlantic crossing. The majority were sold instead to various South American states, though a few were restored to Italy after the war. I must add, however, that between March and July 1941, four ships—*Frisco*, *Mombaldo*, *XXIV Maggio* and *Africana*—reached France from Brazil with valuable cargoes. Other ships, also in burden, came into Bor-

---

[1] Technically, *Eritrea* was a warship, but her speed was so low and her armament so light that she counted as a merchantman for all practical purposes.

deaux or St. Nazaire from Las Palmas, Tenerife or ports in Spain, and the tanker *Fidelitas* from Scandinavia.

All these ships, of course, had to sail alone and unescorted and some of them were lost on the way. The S.S. *Caboto*, for example, scuttled herself in the Persian Gulf to avoid capture; *Ernani* and *Recco* were torpedoed by submarines; *Sangro* fell a victim to an auxiliary cruiser; *Butterfly* was sunk by gunfire off the French coast; and the tanker *Franco Martelli*, with oil from Brazil, was sunk by a submarine just outside St. Nazaire. Most of the crew of this last ship were picked up by a German E-boat and I saw them as they came ashore. They were all suffering from the effects of the oil they had swallowed while in the water, but still more from the bitterness of having lost their ship on the last lap of their 9,000-mile voyage.

This gradual accumulation of Italian ships at Bordeaux set the politicians and the Naval Staff wondering whether they could not be used to keep open trade with Japan. If ordinary cargo boats had run the blockade once, might they not succeed a second and third time? It was an attractive idea, not only because the trade would be useful, but also for the propaganda value of an operation which would demonstrate that the high seas were not, after all, entirely closed to the Axis.

After much debate it was decided to try the experiment of running Italian ships to Japan with mercury, crated aircraft and machine tools on the outward voyage and cotton and rubber on the return voyage. For ships, the M.V. *Himalaya*, which reached France from the Red Sea and Brazil, *Cortellazzo*, *Fusijama* and *Orseolo* were selected. In the end *Fusijama* was unable to leave. *Cortellazzo* cleared from Bordeaux on 29 November 1942, but was attacked by a cruiser and destroyers off the Azores and had to scuttle herself. The *Himalaya* ran into a heavy air attack in the Bay of Biscay and was forced back. The M.V. *Orseolo* (Lt. Tarchiana), however, succeeded in making the double trip across the Atlantic and the Indian

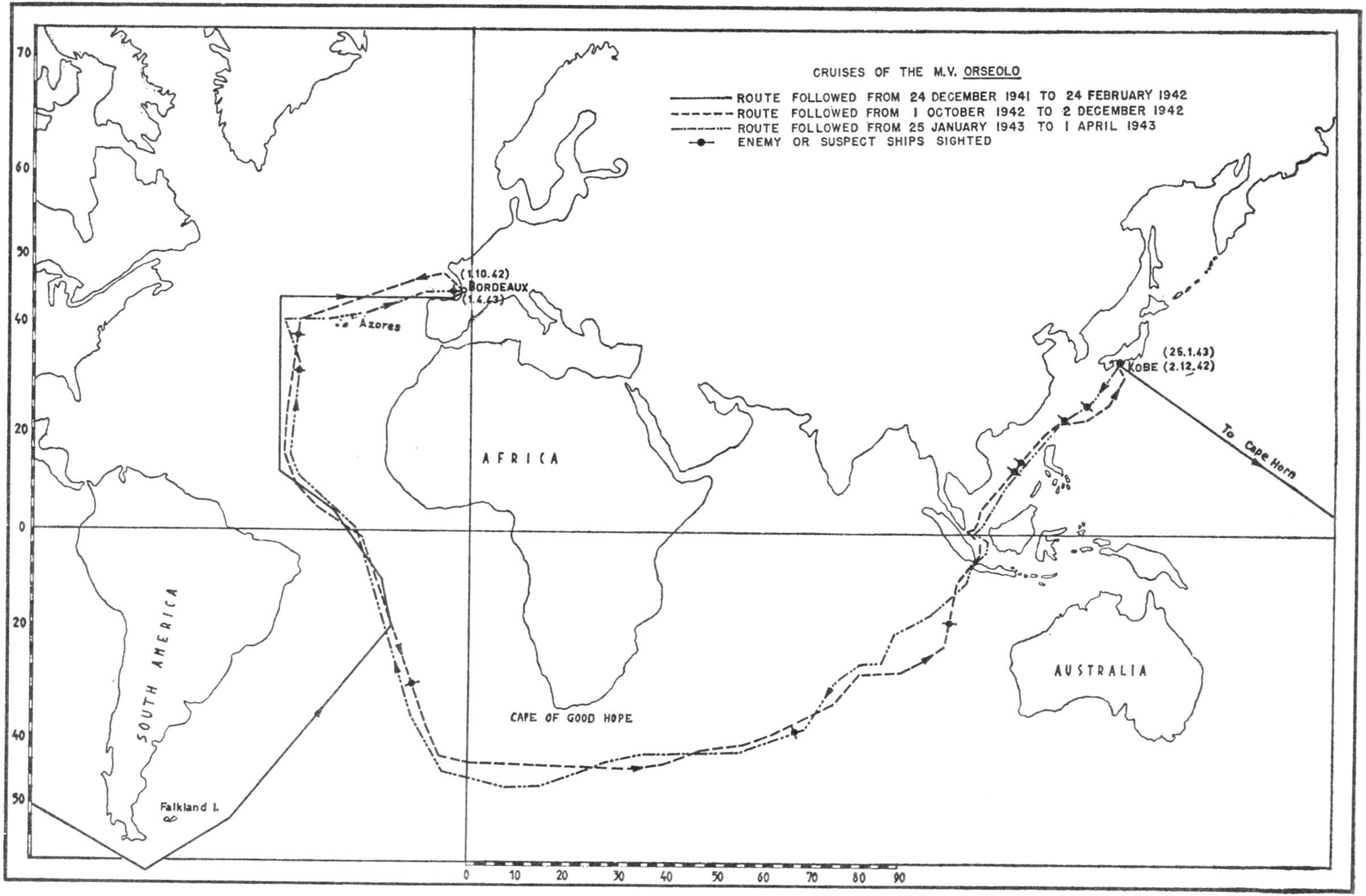
CRUISES OF THE M.V. ORSEOLO
ROUTE FOLLOWED FROM 24 DECEMBER 1941 TO 24 FEBRUARY 1942
ROUTE FOLLOWED FROM 1 OCTOBER 1942 TO 2 DECEMBER 1942
ROUTE FOLLOWED FROM 25 JANUARY 1943 TO 1 APRIL 1943
ENEMY OR SUSPECT SHIPS SIGHTED
(1.10.42)
BORDEAUX
(1.4.43)
Azores
AFRICA
CAPE OF GOOD HOPE
SOUTH AMERICA
Falkland I.
AUSTRALIA
(25.1.43)
KOBE (2.12.42)
To Cape Horn
70
60
50
40
20
0
20
40
50
0
10
20
30
40
50
60
70
80
90

fantry for Albania embarking on Eugenio Di Savoia.

Loading German armored car on an Italian destroyer.

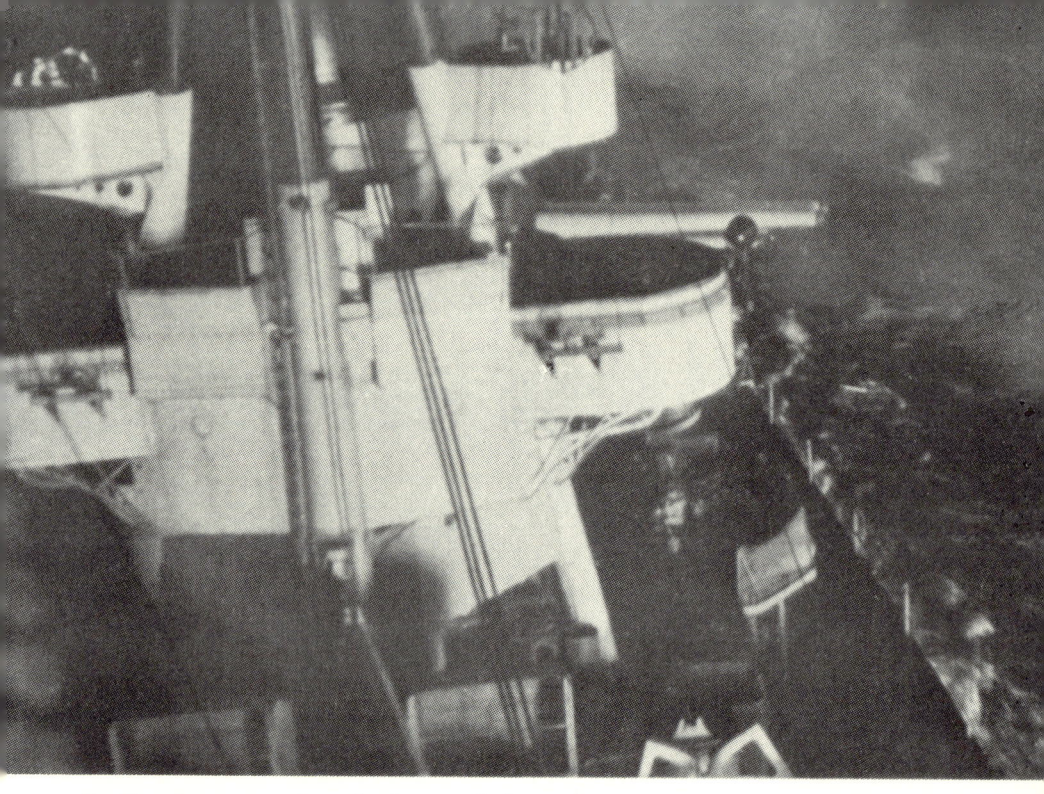

Italian heavy cruiser during a night action.

A cruiser of the Zara class in battle action

Three views of Italian "assault boat."

The dramatic Italian two-man torpedo or "pig."

Blockade Runners

Ocean. She left Bordeaux on 1 October 1942 for Singapore by the Cape route. She reached her destination on 2 December 1942, after a number of adventures, including the sighting of more than one enemy ship, which she avoided by a miracle, and a brush in the China Sea with an American submarine which, however, put herself so close alongside that she was unable to use her armament.

Orseolo left the Far East again on 25 January 1943, with a cargo of rubber and about twenty German soldiers as passengers. She came back by the same route, again sighted enemy ships and again avoided them. The climax came when she was entering the Bay of Biscay and had already picked up her German escort. A patrolling submarine fired three torpedoes at her. She was able to dodge two; but the third blew a great rent in her stern. But *Orseolo* was a tough ship and managed to reach port under her own steam.

The best tribute that one can pay *Orseolo* is to put down the bare figures: 163 days at sea, 54,000 miles covered in waters patrolled day and night by the enemy. With the exception of four German radio operators, all her crew were Italian.

XVII

A Drama in Two Acts

THE setting of this story is the Narrows, the strip of water between Sicily and North Africa, through which no Italian sailor can now pass without uncovering. The story itself is in two sharply contrasted scenes: the first a moonlight night made lurid by explosions, gunflashes and star shells; the second, a silent, almost furtive scene which only the most alert observer would have noticed at all.

The first scene was during one of the many clashes between Italian convoys and British cruisers and destroyers. It took place on the night of 16 April 1941, close under the Kerkennah banks in the Gulf of Gabes; and it ended, like so many similar night actions, with the destuction of the convoy.

On this occasion the convoy and its escort were under the command of Commander Piero De Cristoforo, in *Tarigo*. He had no resemblance at all to the conventional tough hero of films and thrillers, being, on the contrary, fair, slightly built and gentle-mannered. His character matched his appearance; he was a retiring man with the diffident manner which comes from a careful upbringing. Yet at the crisis of his life as a seaman and a fighting man he showed what an indomitable spirit was hidden behind this shy exterior, which seemed so much more charming than vigorous. But it appeared when the time came that De Cristoforo had in fact the heart of a hero, coupled

Drama in Two Acts 123

with a fortitude which still seems barely credible. The answer lay in his deep, almost mystical patriotism.

His career before the war had been much the same as anyone else's. He had served afloat and in campaigns overseas and had had one assignment in the Far East. He had also held the appointment (which usually went to a naval lieutenant) of A.D.C. to H.R.H. the Prince of Piedmont—an honor which he owed as much to his personal and social as to his professional gifts. On his promotion he had to leave the Court at Naples. The outbreak of war found him captain of the *Tarigo* with the rank of commander. She was one of twelve destroyers of the *Navigatori* class which, being old and slow, were used for all kinds of jobs and especially for the dangerous and responsible work of escorting African convoys. You may judge what this meant from the fact that of these twelve ships only one, my own *Da Recco*, was still afloat after the Armistice.

De Cristoforo might well have claimed a better billet—a flotilla leader for example. But he was not the type of man either to wangle anything or to complain. He accepted *Tarigo* as what fate and the Admiralty had given him and took up his duties forthwith.

We must now come back to the early hours of 17 April. It was a calm night with little moon showing; five cargo boats were sailing under the lee of Kerkennah, escorted by *Tarigo* with the destroyers *Lampo* and *Baleno* in company. At two in the morning they were only a few hours' steaming from Tripoli; but this was the most dangerous part of the route, within easy range of Malta, whence British cruisers and destroyers were then operating. And Malta was alert, for a reconnaissance plane had spotted the convoy shortly before midnight. Our ships knew nothing of this; nor was there any action they could have taken if they had known.

The attack developed about two o'clock, the British force coming in from astern on the dark side of the horizon, invisible to our ships, who were clearly silhouetted against the moon. It was a well-planned surprise, delivered at the right moment and from the most favorable angle. How many British ships were there? I do not know exactly[1]—certainly several destroyers, helped out—in the usual British whirlwind technique—by fighters and aircraft dropping flares.

Tarigo was hit at once by a salvo which exploded her magazine and tore her bridge apart. De Cristoforo had his leg blown off, but, as soon as a tourniquet had been applied, he insisted on carrying on and directing operations. *Baleno* and *Lampo* were also hit before they even knew what was happening. All *Baleno*'s officers were killed, including her captain. *Lampo* managed to fire a few rounds from her guns and five torpedoes before, riddled with shot, she ran aground on the Kerkennah reefs. It was all over in a few minutes, or perhaps seconds.

Tarigo, with her commander mortally injured, continued the action at great odds—an old and damaged destroyer against undamaged destroyers, supported by aircraft. But De Cristoforo wanted at all costs to keep the British force engaged so that the remaining ships of the convoy could make good their escape. (One of them, the *Arta*, was in fact able to beach herself.) The odds were now one against four or five and the outcome not difficult to foresee.

It was a heroic fight, for *Tarigo* was drawing the enemy's whole fire. Several officers were killed and casualties among the crew were heavy; but De Cristoforo, with extraordinary determination, kept his ship in action and her remaining 4.7-inch guns firing. The main magazine had already gone; there was a fire in the boiler room, and *Tarigo*, now no more than a smoking wreck, was hove to. Luca Balzofiore, her engineer officer, blinded by the flash of an explosion, had himself led up to the bridge to make his last report to the captain and to die with him.

When the last gun had become silent De Cristoforo was

[1] Actually, the four destroyers of the 14th Flotilla (Capt. P. J. Mack). (Tr.)

Drama in Two Acts 125

still able to summon enough strength to direct the firing of the remaining torpedoes. His orders were carried out by Sub-Lt. Besagno—hardly more than a boy—who was still miraculously unhurt. He behaved with the greatest steadiness and was able to score a direct hit on H.M.S. *Mohawk* and sink her.

That was *Tarigo's* last act of defiance; but one thing remained for her captain, to see to the safety of his ship. He roused out the survivors of his crew to fight the fires, which had now taken serious hold; and they all set to, wounded and uninjured together, among the tangle of battered guns, red-hot metal and wrecked machinery. But the end had come. *Tarigo* turned over and sank, her colors flying and her dying captain at his post. The British ships drew off; and the survivors of *Tarigo, Lampo, Baleno* and *Mohawk* and of the cargo boats *Sabaudia, Adana, Aegina, Arta* and *Isernia* were left in the water to be picked up next morning by the hospital ship *Orlando*.

We now come to the second act, which began in a closely guarded room in the Admiralty and ended at sea. The leading character is a scruffy, smelly trawler such as can be seen on any part of the sea or in any port in war as well as in peacetime; a most innocent, unwarlike boat, at least in appearance. But all kinds of mysterious jobs came to trawlers during the war and even before it, when some countries used them for espionage.

This particular boat snorted and smoked her way to the scene of the action of 17 April. Her ostensible purpose was to fish; and the place she selected, curiously enough, was exactly over the spot, discovered after intensive search, where *Mohawk* had gone down. She placed herself so that no observer on shore could see what she was doing, and then quietly slipped a diver overboard. He remained below far longer than was necessary to clear the screw or free a net from the bottom. . . . The trawler stayed in the same position for three days, keeping up a pretence of fishing, while the diver rummaged *Mohawk's* hull. At last a line drew up a curious, perforated steel box. It was full of books, which were more precious than the richest treasure trove because they contained the *Mohawk's*—and therefore the British Navy's—confidential papers, ciphers and signal procedure. Intelligence officers in a trawler, equipped for a rather specialized kind of fishing, had carried out to perfection the plan hatched in the Admiralty.

The papers in the steel box had been thoroughly soaked by sea water and their jackets damaged; but no one minded that. They still contained invaluable information which enabled us to decipher British naval signals for many months to come. But eventually, the Admiralty in London began to notice that the Italians knew altogether too much. Then it was our turn to start again from the beginning—and so on throughout the war.

XVIII

Da Mosto's Last Fight

THE DESTROYER *Da Mosto* kept up her fire against the British cruisers *Aurora* and *Penelope* until the 4.7-inch guns on her forecastle were awash. Her stern had been blown off by the explosion of the after-magazine and her decks were under water. She could no longer move or steer; and it was only a question of time before she sank. Yet she continued to fight as long as her forward guns were above water: two 4.7-inch guns against the twelve 6-inch of the cruisers and the five 4.7's of their escorting destroyer.

Francesco Dell'Anno, *Da Mosto's* captain, and his crew were fighters of the kind who do not count the cost. They took the view that a battle went on as long as any weapon could be brought to bear or men were still alive to man it. So *Da Mosto* kept her colors flying to then end, when she was no more than a jagged lump of metal, sticking out of the water like a halftide rock. When she finally sank, her three opponents lined their decks and steamed slowly over the spot in a last tribute to the old ship, which had fought so desperately to protect the convoy in her charge.

The word convoy is perhaps misleading in this connection, for *Da Mosto* had only one ship, the tanker *Mantovani*, under her wing. But, as I pointed out earlier this arrangement was not uncommon. The action on 1 December 1941, was not the only occasion when a tanker ran the Narrows with only a single destroyer as escort. Some critics may express surprise at a policy which could send out ships so lightly escorted in broad daylight within a few miles of Malta, which was then in full operation as as offensive base. I offer no comment on this, apart from what has already been said in an earlier chapter. I can only repeat that the battle of the convoys was the bloodiest and most desperate engagement fought by the Italian Navy during the war.

Da Mosto and *Mantovani* were about seventy miles from Tripoli at 1300 hours when the inevitable attack by torpedo bombers burst upon them. *Mantovani* was hit at once and brought to a standstill. But, though unable to move, she was still afloat; and it was still possible—though at great risk—to take her in tow, bring her into port and salvage her cargo. Dell'Anno, after a rapid review of the situation, decided to try. At the second attempt he succeeded in getting a line on board—a difficult maneuver duly recognized in the subsequent citation: "The merchant ship in his charge having been hit and put out of action, he attempted with great professional skill, while under heavy air attack, to take her in tow. . . ." This bald account does less than justice to the occasion. While the aircraft straddled her with bombs and torpedoes *Da Mosto* tried to save what could be saved without any regard for her own safety, and fought back as best she could with her machine guns and her main armament. This strange duel between bombers and a destroyer trying to salvage a tanker, went on for some hours and might even have ended in *Da Mosto's* favor, if *Aurora*, *Penelope* and an enemy destroyer had not appeared on the scene at about 1800 hours.

The position of the Italian ships was now hopeless, for no destroyer could defend herself in daylight against two well-armed light cruisers. *Da Mosto* would have been fully justified in abandoning *Mantovani*, which had now been hit again and was clearly a total loss. But Dell'Anno was not accustomed to disengage without fighting and turned at full speed towards the enemy squadron. Ignoring their heavy fire, he discharged his torpedoes and then altered course under cover of a smoke screen.

He might well have been content with this single attack, since *Mantovani* had now been sunk. But as *Da Mosto* was still undamaged and had not yet fired all her torpedoes, her captain felt it his duty to continue the action. It was no longer a question of the safety of the tanker or even of his own ship, an old veteran of the *Navigatori* class, but simply of a sailor's duty, as Dell'Anno understood it; the duty of fighting to the last.

Da Mosto having failed to score a hit with her first salvo came in to the attack again, closing the range still more, and fired her remaining torpedoes at the enemy. As she was turning back into the smoke, she received several hits aft, which fired the magazine. She was now a wreck, unable to move and an easy prey to the enemy; but she kept up a lively fire until she was actually sinking.

"He was the last to leave his ship as she went down," says the citation for Dell'Anno's Gold Cross.

By an extraordinary chance and much against his will, Dell'Anno was saved on this occasion but his life was in fact over. Three months later, on 23 March 1942, he was lost at sea with the *Scirocco*, having joined her at his own request immediately after the sinking of *Da Mosto*.

XIX

Commander Ignazio Castrogiovanni

No one can read Ignazio Castrogiovanni's log of the battle of Pantelleria without emotion. It describes in the driest of official prose the action fought on 15 June 1942, by two destroyers of his flotilla, *Vivaldi* and *Malocello*. In form it is no more than a bare chronology of events:

0534 hours: Crew called to general quarters.
0550 hours: Opened fire; range about ten miles.
0554 hours: The Admiral (Da Zara, commanding 7th Division) orders an attack on the convoy. We close the enemy, followed by *Malocello*. Four English destroyers turn to intercept us, opening a heavy fire.

You might call this a dull account with no life in it. It does not even call attention to the fact that our ships were outnumbered: *Vivaldi* and *Malocello* (Cdr. Leoni) against four British destroyers, detached from the rest of the escort to head off the Italian attack. Yet it was a noteworthy engagement, which provided a climax to the long-drawn-out battle of Pantelleria.[1]

0558 hours: Explosion observed on board the third destroyer of the enemy formation.

---

[1] Between 11 and 15 June 1942, an attempt was made to run two convoys into Malta from Gibraltar and Alexandria simultaneously. In a running fight lasting four days, both convoys were heavily bombed and attacked by units of the Italian Fleet. The Alexandria convoy of eleven ships was forced back. (Tr.)

Commander Castrogiovanni 131

0559 hours: Range 7,000 yards to merchantmen; 6,000 to destroyers. First torpedo salvo fired. Gunfire directed alternately on destroyer and merchantmen, when later visible through the smoke screen.

A routine report containing no more detail than is needed to convey the facts. But that laconic style was typical of Castrogiovanni, one of the ten or twelve captains who commanded destroyer flotillas during the war. It found its final expression six months later, on 17 December 1942, when he was lost with his latest command, *Aviere*, when she was torpedoed and broken in two by a British submarine. But Castrogiovanni had always had the same vein of austerity even as a young midshipman in 1916, when he found himself in the water after the sinking of the destroyer *Nembo*, but clung to his raft and refused to be rescued by an enemy ship. This incident was commemorated on a gold medal, which the city of Florence wished to present to him and for which D'Annunzio composed the inscription: "We will never truckle to death or the enemy."

Castrogiovanni's approach to life was always the same, whether in the Adriatic in 1916, on convoy duty in the Mediterranean in 1941 and 1942, in the action of Pantelleria or in the Narrows where he met his death.

But let us come back to his log. It records the hits obtained on another destroyer and a merchantman by *Vivaldi* and *Malocello*; then comes this passage:

0620 hours: A shell explodes in the forward engine room. Steam and oil pipes riddled by splinters. Other shell fragments start fire in adjacent main magazine....

At a range of five or six thousand yards—analogous to a pistol duel in Nelson's day—it was inevitable that the Italian ships should be hit sooner or later. What is surprising is that it was only *Vivaldi* that suffered and only to the extent of a single shot. But she was now stationary, with a serious fire on board, within close range of the enemy ships, and under heavy attack from their guns and torpedoes. Nevertheless, she kept up her own rate of fire, even though her main battery had to be operated by hand. When the British destroyer *H68* came so close that the name on her stern could be read, *Vivaldi* fired two torpedoes and forced her to withdraw.

Malocello remained alongside *Vivaldi*. The description of the action in a recent and much-discussed book contains the sentence: "Only two destroyers, *Vivaldi* and *Malocella*, tried to approach the convoy during the English destroyers' attack; but one of them, having received a hit in her engine room, was immobilized and the other retired." May the writer be forgiven for these closing words. *Malocello* did not retire, but stayed with her damaged consort, laid a protective smoke screen and defended her with guns, torpedoes and machine guns against the British destroyers and the aircraft which presently arrived from Malta. Castrogiovanni's log continues in its blunt style:

0645 hours: *Malocello* circles *Vivaldi*, lays smoke and lays down a heavy barrage.

Shortly after seven o'clock the British abandoned their prize and drew off. But there still remains another enemy, the fire below, which threatened *Vivaldi* increasingly for many hours to come. It did not begin to slacken until the afternoon and was not finally brought under control until about ten o'clock that night. The fire crept forward from the engine room toward midships, caused explosions in No. 2 magazine, reached the forward gun turret and spread thence to the ammunition lockers for the machine guns and finally to the oil tanks, from which jets of burning fuel ran along the waterways and over the deck.

But *Vivaldi* did not give up. Castrogiovanni remained calmly at his post, almost in the center of the flames. He asked *Malocello* to send over further supplies of fire-fighting equipment and to take his most serious casualties on board. But the fire was now too fierce to be controlled by any apparatus on *Malocello*, even with the help of *Premuda*, *Oriani* and *Ascari* who had now come up. It was essential to bring *Vivaldi* into Pantelleria, where the equipment at the naval base could be used to smother the flames. But this could not be done until late that evening, though according to Castrogiovanni's log it was still only nine in the morning. They had another twelve hours of fire-fighting before them while explosions took place in the magazine and the enemy from time to time renewed their attack:

0936 hours: Four Swordfish torpedo bombers attack *Vivaldi* and *Malocello*, both hove to, at a range of sixty yards.

0950 hours: A formation of seven bombers over the two ships which reply with intense A.A. fire. A near miss by stick of about thirty bombs on the port quarter.

The burning ship was not taken in tow by *Premuda* until 1020 hours. Then began the slow and difficult trip to Pantelleria, where Castrogiovanni hoped, even if he could not dock his ship, to beach her and prevent her loss. It is at this point that we find the only entry in his log which is not strictly official:

1028 hours: The crew is making untiring efforts to control the fire, regardless of flames and explosions. I am proud of them.

After this one sentence the log takes up its prosaic tale again, with no further mention of the captain's feelings, which can still move us, intense as they must have been. I had always been a friend of Castrogiovannis' and his keen admirer, and felt it deeply when I heard of his death in the same waters in which *Da Recco* had endured so much only a few days before. But it was not until I read the minute-by-minute account in his log that I understood the full measure of his unassuming courage.

The tow to Pantelleria proceeded. The wounded were taken off in hospital boats sent from the naval base and most of *Vivaldi*'s crew put ashore. Only the officers, petty officers and about fifty able seamen remained on board—and, of course, the captain. *Premuda* had the tow and *Malocello* stood by to render help, if necessary. *Ascari* and *Oriani* had both rejoined the 7th Division.

Vivaldi was saved; but she left Pantelleria for Trapani and later Taranto in such a condition that many months were needed to repair her. In fact, the refit lasted for nearly a year and had hardly been completed before she was sunk on 9 September 1943, in action against the Germans off the Straits of Bonifacio.

Castrogiovanni was not a man to stay idle for a whole year. He asked for the command of another flotilla leader and was given *Aviere*. He returned to the escort of Mediterranean convoys, a service in which he acquitted himself so well that, during his whole tour of duty for the summer of 1941 to the end of 1942, no merchant ship and no escort vessel was lost under his command. He escorted dozens of convoys from Italy to North Africa and back again and at various times used his own ship to run urgently needed gasoline to Tobruk or ammunition to Bengazi. He was ambushed by submarines, tracked by radar, lit up by flares and attacked by bombers and torpedo bombers, but emerged triumphantly from it all. This was a distinction which he shared with Galati, who commanded the *Vivaldi* flotilla from 1940 to the summer of 1941, and which he kept until his last voyage on 17 December 1942.

Even on that occasion the S.S. *Ankara* and the destroyer *Camicia Nera* reached Bizerte safely, though *Aviere*, the flagship, was hit by two torpedoes from a patrolling submarine in what was later known to both sides as "death alley," where twenty-one escorts were sunk in three months, to say nothing of submarines, E-boats and merchant ships. The enemy attack developed about 11 a.m. Castrogiovanni put his ship across the track of torpedoes aimed at the *Ankara*. She was hit at once and sank in a few seconds, blown in two, with her bows pointing skyward.

A hundred men or so, the captain among them, found themselves in the water, probably with no clear idea of how they got there. They assembled round a few pieces of floating debris and two Carley floats—big rafts, with ratlines round them, supported by metal buoyancy tanks. The attacking submarine had, of course, disappeared. *Ankara* and *Camicia Nera*, who might have lingered (especially the latter) to pick up survivors, had both withdrawn as fast as possible from what was evidently a danger zone. Nothing remained for the men in the water but their bits of wreckage, the two Carleys and the immense moral support of their captain. "He was calm and imperturbable," said the survivors, "with a word of encouragement for everyone; he said that we would soon be getting our own back."

The men had to struggle against rough seas, the acrid oil in which they were floating, the cold and the biting wind. Castrogiovanni did not only encourage his men but made the only sacrifice left him and gave up his place on the Carley to a seaman whose strength was failing. When the torpedo boats *Calliope* and *Perseo* reached the scene that afternoon, he had disappeared, "completing," in the words of the citation, "by an act of sacrifice a life entirely devoted to his country and his Service."

XX

Commander Enea Picchio

ON HIS arrival at Taranto after a long tour of duty escorting Mediterranean convoys in the summer of 1942, *Saetta's* skipper, Commander Enea Picchio, reported to the captain commanding the escort group and said smiling:

"You know, sir, during this last trip you never gave me any orders or made any signals."

There was no formality about making one's report after these difficult wartime trips. The destroyers and torpedo boats came into their moorings in succession; and their skippers gathered on the quay to discuss their experiences and express their views, pretty freely, about the Admiralty and shore-based authorities in general. These meetings often took place at night after a late return from a trip which might have lasted four or five days on end. Everyone felt the need to talk even more strongly than the universal need for sleep or a drink. It was a necessary release of nervous tension.

There was no formality even when there were noticeable differences of age or rank. We were all living the same life and running the same risks; and almost all of us were inspired by the same enthusiasm. So our official reports turned into conversations and a profitable exchange of ideas, while they were still fresh in our minds.

The captain's reply to Picchio was: "Why should I give

orders or make signals when you do what's necessary on your own?"

They talked for a little longer about their trip—three merchant ships brought safely from Bengazi to Taranto through a succession of air attacks. They agreed that the best plan was always to open fire on aircraft as soon as they were spotted, even at night and even if there was no chance of hitting them. Then they went back to their ships, Picchio as pleased with the captain's comment as if he had been decorated or patted on the back by the Admiralty.

He was a quiet, self-contained man; a good officer, who took the war in the Mediterranean seriously but without fuss. As a lieutenant he had commanded the torpedo-boat *Andromeda* when she was engaged in the arduous duty of escorting convoys from Brindisi to Valona or Durazzo at the time of the Italian war with Greece. He had then been put in charge of the island of Saseno, a more difficult and complex job than it may sound but certainly not one to satisfy a man like Picchio whose ambition was a roving commission in the Mediterranean, the more dangerous the better. On 9 July 1941, he wrote to his sister: "What annoys me most is to be slaving away in a shore job. . . . I'm wearing myself out here and it's driving me nuts. The pen is not (repeat not) my weapon, so I am going to apply for a ship."

His application went forward and was accepted at the beginning of 1942, when he was given command of *Saetta*. She was a small, old and slow destroyer, of the type normally used for escort duty, which the Admiralty fondly believed could be carried out by less efficient ships than those assigned to service with the Fleet. But Picchio, now a lieutenant commander, knew exactly what he was letting himself in for and welcomed it—a job which was responsible, dangerous and exhausting, but essential to the war effort.

Picchio began his service on the North African run, plying

between Brindisi or Taranto and Bengazi, Tripoli or, later, Tobruk, when that port had been recaptured. It was a wearing life, for each convoy, crawling at the speed of its slowest ship, had to fight its way through, and there was no rest even in port with Bengazi and Tobruk under incessant attack by the R.A.F. *Saetta* sailed sometimes as a unit of the escort, sometimes in command and always showed herself equal to the task, whether it was using her meagre armament against the enemy, picking up survivors or acting as a screen for the merchantmen.

There was no doubt of Picchio's success. When *Saetta* had completed her 100th trip, the Commander in Chief, Admiral Iachino, paid her a visit at Taranto to congratulate her captain and crew. But the work went on just the same. Next day *Saetta* sailed again, this time not on convoy duty, but with the task of towing to Bengazi or Tobruk an old submarine of the *Balilla* class, loaded with gasoline and oil. These were curious trips, about which not much has been written, but fully as dangerous as any other and requiring a high standard of seamanship. Ocean-going submarines no longer fit for operations were stripped down to the bare hull, their engines, armament and gear being taken out, and were used as lighters for the transport of fuel. They had two advantages over conventional craft of this kind: they could be towed at a higher speed (fourteen instead of four or five knots); and they were almost invisible on the surface.

In the middle of August 1942, *Saetta* had just reached Bengazi on one of these towing operations, when she received orders to join a convoy sailing for Italy. It consisted of the M.V. *Bixio* and *Sestriere*, *Da Recco* commanding the escort and the torpedo boats *Orione* and *Castore*. It was a good convoy, fast and well-matched. But neither the speed nor the efficiency of the escort saved *Bixio* from receiving two torpedo hits from a submarine off Navarino. This area was one of the worst in the Mediterranean; one could always be certain of finding an enemy submarine lying in wait there. This time, judging from the number of torpedo tracks, there must have been more than one. *Da Recco* laid a pattern of depth charges round *Bixio* and would then have given certain orders to the rest of the escort. But there was no need. *Castore* had already taken *Sestriere* in charge and was hurrying her away from the danger zone; *Saetta* had laid herself alongside *Bixio* and managed with great skill to pass a towline.

Bixio was at least ten times larger than the destroyer; she had been holed by the torpedoes and was making water, so that she was unnaturally heavy and sluggish. Yet Picchio managed to get his tow working, bad weather and the constant danger of submarines notwithstanding. He took the damaged ship into Navarino and, though the distance was only twenty miles, it needed the whole night—about ten hours—to do it.

From Navarino, Picchio wrote to his mother: "A lot of compliments have been flying round the last few days. There has even been talk of putting me in for the Silver Cross. All God's doing; but I think I can say that I did my best, too." The turn of phrase was entirely characteristic—a true reflection of the spirit which upheld him.

For the salvaging of *Bixio* he received a well-earned decoration and was given leave and told to get some rest. But Picchio was no believer in destroyer captains resting while there was a war on and returned to *Saetta* before his leave was up. He wrote to his sister: "I have got back to my proper life and am very fit. The weather is good and we only need the sea to go down a bit. I'm near the end of my sea time (twenty-two months); but if it weren't for Mother, I shouldn't come ashore at all. . . . I don't want to upset the ship's company."

He returned to the old routine of escorting convoys and towing submarine hulks of gasoline, and went on fighting successfully against enemy submarines and aircraft, now more numerous and deadly than ever. On 21 January 1943, while escorting a merchantman from Tripoli to Syracuse, he was spotted by an aircraft but escaped by running in close under Malta, reasoning that that was the last place where anyone would look for him. He proved to be right and brought his convoy in safely. But the war in the Mediterranean was now entering its last phase. The battle had shifted back to the Narrows, where the Italian Navy had lost so many ships in the summer of 1941. Now, one after another, our surviving merchantmen and escort vessels were sunk in the same waters. In the single month of January 1943, the following ships were lost in death alley: SS. *Morandi, Martini, Sportivo, Edda, Saturno, Pozzuoli;* M.V. *D'Annunzio, Amba Alagi, Bertani, Cinzia;* the destroyers and torpedo boats *Aviere, Bersagliere, Corsaro, Bombardiere, Prestinari, Ardente.* Some were sunk by enemy aircraft, submarines or cruisers; others fell foul of the minefields which all the combatants—Italians, Germans, British, even Americans—had sown so freely. But the German-Italian forces in Tunisia had still to be supplied, whatever the cost; and Italian ships still maintained a regular service between Italy and Tunis or Bizerte, regardless of the risk and the losses. When no more merchantmen were available, warships were used to carry men, ammunition and fuel.

On 7 February, *Saetta* reached Bizerte having disembarked some troops and found the tanker, *Thoreshemeir,* waiting to return empty to Naples. A convoy assembled and sailed at dawn two days later. It consisted of the tanker, *Saetta,* and the torpedo boats *Clio, Monsone, Sirio* and *Uragano.* It was the old destroyer's last voyage and Picchio's also; they were both lost on an errand of mercy. It was almost impossible in those days to avoid blundering into an active minefield somewhere in the Narrows. And so it happened in this case: *Uragano,* one of the flanking torpedo boats, struck a mine and had her stern blown off, so that she was left helpless.

According to the official report this occurred at 0938 hours precisely and the set of the current drove *Uragano* further and further into the minefield. The rest of the convoy, as was proper, carried on and cleared these dangerous waters. But Picchio decided that *Uragano* could not be abandoned and took his own ship into the minefield in an attempt to tow her clear. The report does not say much about what happened next; and we do not even know for certain whether Picchio succeeded in getting a line on board the damaged torpedo boat. We are only told that twelve minutes later, at 0950 hours, *Saetta* also struck a mine. The explosion took place directly amidships and broke her in two, so that she began to sink at once. Picchio was unhurt. The letter of proceedings and the citation for his posthumous Gold Cross both testify that he upheld the highest traditions of the Service. Having given orders to abandon ship and satisfied himself that no one was still on board, he returned to the bridge, unwilling to desert *Saetta* in which he had served so long. The men in the boats saw him salute the colors as she went down.

Such was the death of one whom his fellow officers described as "one of the ablest, bravest and most dashing destroyer captains that Italy ever had."

Part 4. FOUR BRAVE MEN

XXI

Admiral Carlo Bergamini

No one will ever know what happened in the control tower of the *Roma* on the afternoon of 9 September, 1943, when the German air attack burst on her, because all the persons present, from Admiral Bergamini downwards, were lost with the ship. Only one thing is certain: that the admiral had no thoughts for himself, for his distant family or for anything but the ships and men under his command.

Perhaps Bergamini, with his great faith in naval gunnery and the strength of the 35,000-ton battleships, which were in a sense his own creation, never even considered the possibility that one or two bombs from an aircraft might destroy these enormous ships. Even if he did, it was certainly not his own fate which preoccupied him. The last message from the flagship was a faint radio signal: "We are in danger," and then, after a pause, "mortal danger." But these words, sent immediately before the final explosion, were not dictated by the admiral, who would never have authorized a cry for help in such faltering terms. His own last word was the flag signal ordering a change of formation, which *Roma* was still flying when she went down, as if in evidence of the admiral's intense determination to do whatever was possible for the safety of his fleet.

Carlo Bergamini was outstanding among his countrymen for his gifts of leadership. He was also a man of great technical knowledge who left his mark on the new Fleet, which was built up almost from scratch between the wars. (His work on gunnery development was eagerly followed in France and England). But his greatest and best remembered attribute was his deep humanity, which the responsibilities of high command never smothered or weakened. As Admiral Iachino says of him: "He was a modest, unflamboyant man, though not without ordinary professional ambition, calm in times of stress and naturally magnanimous, with no malice or vernom and a great sympathy for human weakness. . . . He had a strong hold on the affections of the lower deck. His men looked on him as a father and would have followed him anywhere."[1]

I remember him when he was in command of the cruiser *Bande Nere* during the Abyssinian war. He seldom went ashore, but spent each evening in port seeing anyone who asked for an interview, whether for advice in some difficulty or simply to spend a few moments with him. They were all his sons—petty officers or young seamen; and it was always as a father that he led them. Even as commander in chief, he never dealt with officers or men as entries on a nominal roll, but invariably as human beings, men or boys whom he knew and whose strengths and weaknesses he understood. He had the same feeling for his ships, which he loved like living creatures and cherished, not only in their paint and brasswork, but as fighting units, able to protect those who sailed in them.

He spent much more time afloat than on shore at technical or administrative posts. Any crisis was sure to find him at sea, as he was during the Abyssinian war or again during the whole

[1] V. Angelo Iachino: *Le due Sirti.*

period from 1940 to 1943. At the outbreak of the late war he was in command of the battle squadron which included the two 35,000 tonners, *Littorio* and *Vittoroi Veneto*, both newly commissioned. (No one was better qualified than Bergamini to bring these ships, the Navy's main strenth, to a state of fighting efficiency.) At the time of the action off Calabria he wanted to take them to sea, though they were not yet shaken down, and offer battle to Cunningham, who was then standing in boldly for the Ionian Sea. The most stringent orders from the Admiralty were needed to veto this plan. In the circumstances these orders were prudent and sensible; whether they were wise is another matter. A seemingly reckless decision sometimes decides the issue of a battle or even a war; and it may well be that the whole course of future events would have been different if, on 9 July 1940, Cunningham had been caught between the fires of Campioni's squadron and Bergamini's capital ships, even though the latter were not yet fully efficient.

At the beginning of 1941, Bergamini, who had been appointed second-in-command to Admiral Iachino, was flying his flag in *Duilio*. In her he carried out a series of convoy operations at great risk, for the old battleship when serving as an escort made a sitting (and much sought after) target for submarines and aircraft. But, so far as I remember, no ship was lost on any of these operations. This was partly the result of an effective defense, based on *Duilio's* heavy armament, and partly on Bergamini's capacity for inspiring the officers and men under his command—perhaps even the ships themselves.

Nevertheless Bergamini missed his chance at any major engagement which would have made his name. He carried out a number of difficult operations with unvarying success; but they never brought him into action with any enemy's main fleet, even after he had succeeded Iachino as commander in chief. It was almost as if Providence had denied him a battle in order to preserve him for the hardest and most painful task of all—that of carrying out the terms of the Armistice.

He knew very little about the matter beforehand. Although he was the head of an efficient fighting service, no one bothered to tell him about General Castellano's mission[1] or to give him any information—still less consult him—about the Navy's intended role in the Armistice. The first that he heard of it was on 7 September at a commanding officers' meeting at the Admiralty, when the Minister, De Courten, without being able to say very much, threw out some hint about the result of the talks at Cassibile between the British and Italian Governments. After the meeting Bergamini returned to Spezia, to resume his command on the *Roma*. The news that the Armistice was to become effective from 8 September reached him by telephone, as did the skeleton orders which were all, in the chaos of the time, that he ever received.

Bergamini had trained the Fleet for battle, not for an Armistice or a voyage to Malta. His reaction, when he heard the news, must have been appalling; but he had the strength of mind to master it. He assembled his admirals and subordinate commanders and addressed them—and through them their ship's companies—at two meetings on board *Roma*, the first on the afternoon of the 8th, the second at about ten o'clock that night. At both meetings—more especially the evening one—he told them what he knew of the course of events. He said that the Armistice provided for the transfer of the whole Italian Fleet to a port controlled by the Allies, but that they would not be required to haul down their flags. He added that no ship should be allowed to fall into the hands of any other Power; if there were no other means of preventing it, they should be scuttled. He then said a few words, spoken from a

---

[1] General Castellano was the Italian representative in the secret negotiations with Allied Force Headquarters, which preceded the Armistice. (Tr.)

full heart, about the dark hour through which Italy was now passing, and finished by saying that he had reached an oral agreement with the Admiralty that for the moment the Fleet should proceed, not to an enemy port, but to La Maddalena,[1] there to await further orders.

Bergamini spoke at once as a leader and the father of his men, as an officer acting under orders and, above all, as a great Italian, who knew how to put into clear and vigorous language what his hearers already felt in their hearts. His eyes were glistening as he spoke and his hands, usually so restless, were quiet.

On the night of 8 September all ships ready for sea left harbor under the Admiral's command, in good order and with their lights blacked out, as they had so often done when going into action. There sailed from Spezia: the battleships *Roma*, flying Admiral Bergamini's flag, *Italia* (ex *Littorio*) and *Vittorio Veneto*; the cruisers *Eugenio di Savoia* (Admiral Oliva), *Montecuccoli* and *Regolo*; the destroyers *Legionario*, *Velite*, *Mitragliere*, *Oriani*, *Artigliere*, *Grecale*, *Fuciliere*, *Carabiniere*, *Da Noli*, *Vivaldi*; and a few torpedo boats. From Genoa sailed the cruisers *Garibaldi* (Admiral Biancheri), *Duca degli Abruzzi* and *Duca di Aosta*.

Only badly damaged ships, such as *Gorizia* and *Bolzano*, or ships under repair remained at Spezia. All the rest set a course to take them west of Corsica and Sardinia; all, that is, except the two destroyers *Da Noli* and *Vivaldi*. They were under orders for Civitavecchia on a mission of which little has been said but which, had it succeeded, might yet have changed the history of those troubled days.

The plan, evolved by De Courten, was for *Da Noli* and *Vivaldi* to carry the King and the Government across to Sardinia, so that the island, fortified by their presence and that of the Fleet, might continue to exert an influence on Italy's

[1] The fleet anchorage in the extreme north of Sardinia. (Tr.)

destinies. The plan, opposed by the Allies, was in any case forestalled by a German occupation of La Maddalena in the early hours of 9 September. The two destroyers, after the loss of the *Roma*, altered course for the Straits of Bonifacio to pick up survivors from the flagship.

During the night of the 8th the ships from Spezia and Genoa joined company and the whole fleet, in line ahead, having rounded Cape Corse, steered for Cape Testa (on the northern point of Sardinia) with the intention of entering La Maddalena from the west. But at about three o'clock in the afternoon, just when this change of course had been completed, a signal from Rome informed Bergamini that German troops were already on the island. The stage was thus set for the last act of the drama. The port for which he was making being closed to him, the admiral altered course again to seaward. But what was to follow? We have no evidence from which to judge Bergamini's intentions. He may have planned to make for some other Italian port, though there was none in the central Mediterranean which could accommodate the whole fleet, or to head for Bône towards the British ships. But perhaps he never came to a final decision, for events overtook him suddenly and tragically, as soon as he had altered course.

At that very moment, shortly after three o'clock, a formation of five German Junkers 77 was sighted, heading for the three batleships. This striking force, armed with guided missiles of a new type,[1] pressed their attack with great determination. All the A.A. guns in the Fleet replied; and Bergamini ordered an immediate change of formation to confuse the enemy and disturb his aim. Nevertheless, *Italia* was hit, though not very seriously, and *Roma* was hit twice, once in the boiler room and once between her forward 15-inch turret and the bridge.

An ordinary bomb would probably have been stopped by the protective armor after penetrating the upper and main

---

[1] The Fritz I, invented by Max Kramer, now in the U.S.

decks; but this special missile passed straight through into the bowels of the ship and exploded in the magazine. The rest of the fleet saw *Roma's* control tower crumple as if it had been paper and a flame as tall as a house shoot up in its place. They saw the battleship falter and then break completely in two. Both halves sank within a matter of minutes or even seconds, after rising nearly upright in the water.

Fifteen hundred men of the *Roma's* crew went down with her and nearly all her officers, including Admiral Bergamini and his chief of staff, Rear Admiral Stanislao Caracciotti. It was all over in less than thirty minutes from the start of the attack.

Rear Admiral Romeo Oliva then assumed command of the Fleet. He ordered the cruiser *Regolo*, the destroyers *Mitragliere* and *Carabiniere* and the torpedo boat *Pegaso* to remain on the scene to pick up survivors, and the other ships to set a southerly course. At dawn on 10 September he made the general signal which has passed into the history of those unhappy days: "H.M. the King commands us loyally to execute the terms of the Armistice, which ensure that our ships shall remain under the Italian flag."

All the units of the Fleet then hoisted the black flag, which was the agreed recognition signal for Italian ships proceeding to Malta.

XXII

Carlo Fecia Di Cossato

An anecdote will serve to show why Carlo Fecia Di Cossato was so much beloved by the men of his two wartime commands, the submarine *Tazzoli* and the torpedo boat *Aliseo*. Indeed, his influence went beyond these two ships and could be felt throughout the submarine fleet and the light forces in general. This particular story about him may seem unimportant by contrast with his operational successes in the Atlantic or at Bastia; but it helps to explain why the torpedo boat crews at Taranto, Brindisi and Augusta supported him in the summer of 1944 against all the persuasion and authority which the Admiralty could bring to bear. But I will go into that tale presently. For the moment I am only concerned with the character of the man, as revealed in the following anecdote.

In August 1941 Di Cossato was commanding *Tazzoli* in the Atlantic and had already started on that long list of successes which made him the most famous of our submarine commanders. *Tazzoli's* billet was in tropical waters and, when they were more than a month out, one of the torpedo men had heatstroke during a heavy spell of work. It turned out later that he had been sick for some time, but had kept quiet about it for fear of missing the trip. He had gone on working normally until the moment when the hot, damp atmosphere of the torpedo compartment was too much for him and he collapsed. The skipper would not allow him to be put in a bunk on the mess deck, but had him moved aft to the tiny space which served as his own cabin. By doing so, he said good-by to the two or three hours' rest in the twenty-four which he had so far allowed himself; but it seemed to him only reasonable that a sick man should have such comforts as were available.

This was the normal attitude of this lieutenant commander, so slight and boyish in appearance, but with a courage which few have equalled. It explains why, when *Tazzoli* had to leave on a special mission in December 1941, with only half her crew, there was almost a mutiny among those who had to stay behind. It had nothing to do with the nature of the mission, which in any case they did not know. It was simply a protest against their skipper's act of sailing without them. They objected to being separated from him, even though missing the trip meant nothing worse than a rest, a soft life at Bordeaux and the avoidance of considerable risk and discomfort.

Di Cossato had only taken command of *Tazzoli* in March, after doing a couple of patrols in her by way of apprenticeship, but he had already established that indissoluble bond with his men which was to make her a record-breaking boat. By December she had already sunk a cruiser, four cargo boats and two tankers and had shot down a Blenheim in the mouth of the Gironde. Of these feats the most difficult had been the sinking of the tanker *Alfred Olsen*, 8,000 tons, which involved a forty-eight hours chase and the firing of all the remaining torpedoes—*Tazzoli* had been a month at sea—and about a hundred rounds of 4.7-inch ammunition.

In the following year *Tazzoli* had an even greater success, so that when Di Cossato finally left submarines in February 1943 he had more than 100,000 tons of enemy shipping to his credit, not including the cruiser. But this is not the place for a detailed account of his war service. It is enough to add that, however bitterly he fought, it was always with humanity. Though he gave no quarter to merchantships, alone or in convoy, there was nothing wanton about his attacks. No shot and no torpedo was fired that was not strictly necessary; and no damaged ship was finished off until he was certain that all the crew were clear. Di Cossato always did his best to provide for survivors, even to the extent of taking the injured on board. Among others he rescued an American sergeant who, after he had been put ashore at Bordeaux, wrote a letter which is reprinted in Antonio Maronari's splendid book *Un sommergible non è tornato alla base:* "I should like to thank the officers and men of *Tazzoli* for their kindness and attention to us while we were on board.... I hope Americans treat your fellows equally well. I am also writing on behalf of the others. With thanks and best wishes. John Oliver Leroy."

At the end of February 1943 the Admiralty decided that Di Cossato should leave submarines and *Tazzoli* go into dock for a long refit. Both decisions were necessary. *Tazzoli,* now known to her crew as "the old suitcase," was worn out by the many thousands of miles that she had sailed and the attacks that she had suffered from depth charges and aircraft, while Di Cossato, after twenty-two months of continuous patrols (some lasting more than two months) in the Mediterranean and the Atlantic, was in urgent need of rest. But his ideas of what constitutes rest were evidently peculiar, for he applied at once for the command of an escort vessel in the Mediterranean. He was given *Aliseo* and the 4th Torpedo Boat Flotilla—all new boats built during the war for escort duty. In 1942 they had worked with the Tunisian convoys and were subsequently used, after the fall of Tunis and Bizerte, to escort German and Italian merchantmen between Italy, Corsica and Sardinia.

On 8 September 1943, Di Cossato was at Bastia with *Aliseo* and her consort *Ardito,* waiting to escort the M.V. *Humanitas* to Spezia that night. It was a perfectly normal operation, which might have ended like so many in an aircraft or submarine attack. It ended instead in a hand-to-hand fight with the Germans, which was one of the few bright episodes—the brightest of all, perhaps—in those unhappy days.

Like most other Italians, Di Cossato and his crew heard the news of the Armistice on the radio on the afternoon of the 8th. It came as a shock to them. Having received no orders, Di Cossato recalled those men who were ashore and made ready to leave harbor with *Aliseo* and *Ardito* at midnight. *Aliseo* cast off first, following the naval custom by which the flotilla leader is always the last in and the first away. The town was quiet and there was no reason to expect anything out of the ordinary. No one could have foretold that a few minutes later the Germans would open first on the Italian ships, or rather on *Ardito*, for *Aliseo* was already clear of the harbor. Perhaps the Germans reacted instinctively to the news of the Armistice or were carrying out orders already received; or perhaps it was the silent departure of the torpedo boats which gave the alarm. At all events, as *Ardito* was getting under way, she became the target of a deadly shell and machine gun fire from the shore batteries and, more particularly, from the ships berthed along the quay. This unexpected fire at close range caused a number of casualties and did enough damage to force *Ardito* back to her moorings.

Di Cossato, already at sea, guessed what was happening and prepared his reply. It was probably an instinctive move rather than a carefully thought out plan. In the Atlantic it had always been his instinct which showed him the best way to dodge the escort and sink a merchantman. So now the same impulse told him that his best chance was to stay outside the harbor and wait for dawn. He spent the night off Bastia with his gun crews manning the three 4.7-inch guns and six machine guns which made up *Aliseo's* armament. So they stood by, waiting for what he felt was bound to happen.

About 7 a.m. on 9 September the German ships—one destroyer, one gunboat and eight landing craft—began to come out of the harbor. *Aliseo* sank them all at the cost of a few

"Pig" base in hold of Olterra at Algeciras, Spain.

The submarine Brin *which served during the entire war.*

A Mediterranean convoy workhorse, the Da Rec

Carlo Fecia Di Cossato   153

scratches. After the action, Di Cossato stayed on the scene to pick up survivors and did, in fact, pick them all up, even the obstinate one who disdained to be rescued.

From Bastia, *Aliseo* proceeded to Portoferraio in Elba, where she arrived on the afternoon of the 9th, just as all the other Italian light forces from the northern Mediterranean were coming in—torpedo boats, corvettes, gunboats, M.T.B. Some had come of their own accord and some under orders from Admiral Aimone di Savoia Aosta or Admiral Nomis di Pollone. And, once there, they all sat down to wait, among them *Ardito*, which had followed on from Bastia after temporary repairs.

That day at Portoferraio there was much wavering and indecision. It was not provoked by the political implication of the Armistice, but solely by the fear that its terms might oblige our ships to haul down their flags. Seamen, who had never hesitated to face the enemy and had gone into battle with joy and enthusiasm, now showed a resolute refusal to accept the Armistice until they had received an official guarantee on this point. They regarded their own fate as secondary to that of the flag.

On the 10th, however, the torpedo boats *Aliseo, Ardimentoso, Fortunale, Ariete, Indomito, Calliope* and *Animoso* left Elba for Palermo en route to Malta, but only because they had by then received direct orders from the King, supported by a statement in writing from Admiral Nomis di Pollone that "the terms of the Armistice do not include the surrender of our ships or the hauling down of the flag."[1] On these two conditions—the King's order and the Admiral's promise—they set sail for Malta. Di Cossato, now a commander, was the senior officer of the group, and it was he who urged officers and men to carry out their orders. But he also proposed that charges should be laid in the magazines, ready to explode if our ex-enemies went

---

[1] The fourth clause in the Armistice signed on 3 September read: "Immediate transfer of the Italian Fleet and Italian aircraft to such points as may be designated by the Allied C. in C., with details of disarmament to be prescribed by him." (Tr.)

back on their undertaking. Later, at Malta, when the rumor went round that part of the Fleet was to be handed over to other countries, Di Cossato gave the following order to the ships of his flotilla: "If the order to hand over our ships is confirmed, wherever you may be, fire all your torpedoes and all the ammunition you have on board into the ships around you, so as to remind the Allies that promises must be respected. After that, if you are still afloat, scuttle yourselves."

The spirit in which Di Cossato faced the Armistice shows clearly through these words. He obeyed orders scrupulously because they were given in the King's name, and he was not a man lightly to disregard the oath of allegiance which he had taken at the age of seventeen, when he first entered the Navy. In the same spirit he carried out the escort duties which the Allies assigned to *Aliseo;* but when an admiral expatiated on the advantages of co-belligerency, he answered drily that he had no interest in politics and was only carrying out His Majesty's orders.

In the chaos of the ensuing months Di Cossato had only one thing to hold on to; and it was inevitable that, when a new Government was formed at Salerno in 1944, which refused the oath of loyalty to the Crown, his long-suppressed personal feelings should erupt violently. He refused to recognize the Government or carry out its orders and informed the admiral commanding at Taranto that *Aliseo* would not sail on escort duty the following day as ordered. Di Cossato's opinions were always clear and firmly stated. Moreover, as his English and German opponents knew, it was extremely difficult to shift him. Argument by his brother officers and pressure from above were both equally useless once he had made up his mind. Even an interview with the Chief of the Naval Staff, who was known for his loyalty to the House of Savoy, produced no result. Di Cossato answered him as he had the others: that a Government not in allegiance to the King was unconstitutional and that its orders could not to be obeyed because they had no legal validity.

There was nothing for the Admirality to do but to relieve him of his command and put him under close arrest for three months in the castle at Taranto. For an ordinary commander, however brave and well-liked, the penalty would probably have been more severe. But this was Carlo Di Cossato, the idol of his men, who had no intention of allowing their flotilla captain, their leader *par excellence*, to be put on the beach or punished. The whole town was in an uproar. Slogans supporting Di Cossato appeared on walls and even on the steps of the house where the Minister of Marine was staying; and naïve plans were made to rescue him by force from the castle.

As the result he was released, having been dismissed from the Service, and went to Naples to stay with a friend. Outwardly he was calm and composed and seemed to be looking about for some civilian job; but something had snapped in his heart. He evidently felt that the Italy for which he had fought with such legendary courage had finally disintegrated. No doubt, too, the current atmosphere of compromise and cynical time-serving disgusted him; and he began to be conscious, perhaps for the first time, of the full weight and humiliation of defeat.

On 2 September 1944, at the age of thirty-six, he put an end to a life which had become meaningless. He left a note for the friend with whom he was staying: "Please forgive me for doing this in your house, but my own is the other side of the lines and it is not a thing which I can do with decency in the street. If anyone asks why, say that friendship, success and an income are not everything. To go on living one must have something more, which I have lost. On the brink.... Cossato."

XXIII

Human Torpedoes

I

Referring to Malta's reaction to the attack by Italian naval assault forces on the night of 25 July 1941, a British Admiral wrote among other things: ". . . the fire from the defenses lasted two minutes. Then there was silence: there was no one left to shoot at. When dawn came the guns found two more targets and destroyed them."

Luck went so much against the Italians on that occasion, and the disaster was so complete, that two minutes were enough to destroy their whole force. All the pilots engaged were killed or captured and the headquarters staff of 10th Flotilla MAS, which planned and carried out the operation, was practically annihilated. The two force commanders, Moccagatta and Giobbe, Captain Falcomatà, the medical officer, and the E-boat commander, Lt. Parodi, all died that morning. Two of the pilots, Carabelli and Pedretti, deliberately sacrificed their lives; and Lt. Cdr. (E) Tesei was blown up by the charge which he had laid himself and which he had voluntarily given an instantaneous fuse.

Tesei, the inventor and perfecter of submarine assault craft, had been nicknamed "the angel of death," because he regarded every operation primarily as a moral exercise. He was a native of Marina di Campo in Elba and a born seaman; but his greatest love was for his country, to which he gave not only his keen intelligence and technical ability but his whole being. He used to say: "It is not the outcome of a particular operation or even the whole war that matters. What is needed is men who are willing to sacrifice themselves so that future generations, inspired by their example, may have the strength to conquer." These words were Tesei's profession of faith, the gospel of a man to whom war was the ultimate test of a nation's moral fiber. Elios Toschi, perhaps his closest friend and intimate, writes this of him: "Tesei lives in a different world and by another scale of values—an exalted one but too sublime, too speculative. He believes that in war one must go on acting all the time, never counting the cost, never worrying about victory, because victory itself is unimportant...."

War is not made, still less won, by "ifs," so it is useless to speculate what might have happened if Italy had begun hostilities with a surprise attack by a hundred or more assault craft against British Mediterranean bases. Yet I may be allowed to dally with the idea for a moment, because this was the plan formed by Tesei in 1929, when he and Elios Toschi drew the first sketches for the human torpedo or S.L.C. I heard about the plan from a close friend of Tesei—a senior officer, much older than he was—who told me that the original designs for this ingenious and deadly weapon had been submitted in 1929, when Tesei was still an engineer-sub-lieutenant. At that time war with England did not seem even remotely probable; and the schemes of Tesei and Toschi had no precise objective beyond that of strengthening our naval armament. It was not until 1935 and the years following, when the Abyssinian War had made a clash between England and Italy inevitable, that they found their real purpose and direction.

Tesei believed, like many other naval officers, that Italy's limited resources and small industrial potential gave her no chance of victory, unless she succeeded in knocking out the

British fleet by a surprise attack at the very beginning of the war. As far back as 1935, Tesei and Toschi had calculated that a hundred human torpedoes, despatched to enemy bases in thirty suitably equipped submarines, and then piloted through the boom defences to the ships selected for mining, would be enough to cripple the enemy's fleet for many months. No one can say what would have happened if this project had been carried out. Something like it was done by the Japanese when they attacked Port Arthur in 1904 and again at Pearl Harbor on 7 December 1941—with startling success on both occasions. I may also quote, perhaps, from the American naval periodical, the *O.N.I. Review*, for January 1946: "It is the opinion of many English officers that if the Italian Admiralty had made unlimited use of its assault forces, specially of 'human torpedoes,' and had employed them immediately they came into the war, the Mediterranean Fleet would have been seriously reduced. With massive attacks at Gibraltar, Malta and Alexandria, it is possible that Italy would immediately have gained complete control of the Mediterranean."

II

Tesei's plans were originally formed, as I have said, in 1929, though only in outline. He put them forward again in greater detail in 1936, when he and Toschi had completed the design of their craft and built a prototype, powered by the motor from an old elevator. But neither then nor later was their work taken as seriously as it deserved, owing to the innate conservatism and lack of imagination, which have always been the greatest weakness of our Naval Staff. Between 1936 and 1940 trials, experiments and training went forward on a small scale. But Tesei and Toschi continued to improve the combined submarine and torpedo which they had invented and even built with their own hands in time snatched from their duties as engineer-officers in antiquated submarines. When war broke out they claimed the right to be first to try the new weapon against the enemy. There were many objections and difficulties, which Toschi has described in his book: "The Captain of Submarines (at Spezia) was standing beside his desk talking on the telephone to Submarine Command in Rome. It was a long, tense conversation: on one side a man who knew the form, could see how determined I was, and wanted to use his manpower to the best advantage; on the other a bureaucrat in difficulties who ... didn't want to give way."

Where Tesei is concerned, we have no personal record. But his sisters have given their help in reconstructing his short life, and his brother-in-law, Engineer Admiral Carlo Matteini, has made available a number of letters written by Tesei before the Alexandria, Gibraltar and Malta operations. In these intimate letters, full of his hopes and fears, he often quotes St. Augustine on the power of the spirit as the only means of progress.

We also owe to Admiral Matteini another incident which illustrates the selfdenial that Tesei practiced from the very beginning of his career. The Admiralty made an award to the inventors of the S.L.C. of a Gold Medal, First Class, for their contribution to naval science, and the sum of 15,000 lire. The two officers accepted the medal, but refused the money on the ground that a cash-value could not be given to work done purely from patriotic motives. But the Admiralty, having once allocated the money, could not take it back and the argument dragged on until the outbreak of war and after. Before he left on the Alexandria operation, Tesei arranged with Matteini to draw the money, if he did not come back, and divide it among the fitters who had worked on the project. But in fact Tesei did return after a trying ordeal and the award remained in an Admiralty suspense account until the Under Secretary decided to close an awkward file by expropriating it.

Tesei's first operation, carried out in the second half of August 1940, was against Alexandria. This was the first trial of the new weapon. The pilots of the human torpedoes were Tesei, Toschi, Franzini and Birindelli, with Durand de La Penne in reserve. The approach was to be made in the submarine *Iride* under Brunetti's command from a starting point in the little bay of Menelao in the Gulf of Bomba, not far from the Egyptian frontier. However, the operation came to a tragic end before it had really started. On 22 August *Iride* was torpedoed by three British aircraft. She was to have left for Alexandria that evening and already had the "pigs" and some of the pilots on board. She had come out of harbor about midday to carry out a necessary practice-dive.

Iride was hit at the level of the gun platform and sank rapidly. Some of her crew were killed outright by gunfire or the explosion of the torpedoes; others, who were on the bridge, found themselves in the water more or less seriously injured. A certain number were trapped in the submarine when she sank, and might or might not be alive. No one could tell until later; but the pilots, led by Tesei, dived at once (without either diving suits or breathing apparatus, which were both on *Iride*) to examine the submarine, lying on her side about eleven fathoms down, to see if anything could be done. They carried out long dives, first with no aids and then with oxygen masks sent urgently from Tobruk, and discovered that nine men were still alive in the stern compartment. Tesei even managed to talk to them. By some odd trick of acoustics they could hear his voice clearly if he spoke into the small air space formed by a hand held in front of his mouth. He encouraged them and gave them detailed instructions how to use the after escape hatch. He then worked till he was exhausted clearing the hatch, which had been jammed by the wrenching of the hull.

Tesei worked for twenty hours on end, constantly under water, with the result that he damaged his nasal membrane and brought himself to the point of collapse. But he did not give up until the survivors from *Iride* reached the surface. Two petty officers had died while trying to force open the hatch before it was cleared; and one seaman died soon after reaching the surface. But six men were snatched from death by the determination of the divers. Four of the "pigs" on board *Iride* were also recovered.

At this point Tesei realized that there was still something missing—the ensign which the submarine was flying when she sank. Despite his exhaustion he dived again and brought up the small, discolored square of bunting. This may seem hardly worth mentioning; but it is small incidents like this—or his refusal of the prize money—which bring out Tesei's character most clearly.

On 16 July, just before the Alexandria operation, he had written to Matteini: "My dear Carlo, There's no need for chatter or word-spinning. We have always understood each other and you know what I mean even if I don't say it. Let us hope to God that the day may soon come when all this planning will lead to action. Yours ever, Tesei." These words exemplify his feverish desire for action and his impatience with the way in which the war was being run.

III

The peak of Tesei's wartime career was the attack on Malta. I shall say something of that rash, unhappy venture in a moment; but first I must give some account of Tesei's life between August 1940 and July 1941.

In the middle of September 1940, less than a month after his salvage work in the Gulf of Bomba, he sailed with Borghese on *Sciré* for an operation against Gibraltar, which, however, was cancelled on orders from the Admiralty. A second attempt was made at the end of October. There were four pairs of pilots: Tesei and Pedretti, Birindelli and Paccagnini, Durand de La Penne and Bianchi, with Bertozzi and Viglioli in reserve. But once more they were dogged by bad luck and cheated of the prize which their boldness deserved. *Sciré* carried out her part brilliantly and excellent work was done by Durand de La Penne and Birindelli, the latter being the first Italian to surmount the defences of Gibraltar and force his way into the harbor. But Tesei's trip was a perfect martyrdom.

He left *Sciré* about 2:30 a.m. on 30 October, but did not reach the northern entrance of the harbor until five. This was partly because his "pig" was not running well, but mainly because he had to make continual alterations of course to avoid the ships of a large convoy, which had chosen that night to sail from Gibraltar. In all it took two and a half hours' hard work, complicated by the difficulty of maneuvring his sluggish and unstable craft, by underwater charges thrown from the guard boats, and by the congested traffic of ships and tugs. The physical strain was heavy enough to cause serious damage to Tesei's heart. But it was not this which made him abandon the operation just as he was about to reach the boom, so much as the practical question of the timetable. It was already five o'clock and too late to complete the operation before dawn. Moreover, the "pig" was no longer holding her trim and the breathing apparatus—both Tesei's and his No. 2's—were giving trouble. If they had carried on, they would certainly have been discovered and would have compromised the other pilots, of whose success nothing was then known. Tesei turned back and landed at La Linea at seven-thirty, after five hours in the water.

La Penne was also obliged to give up at the boom for much the same reasons as Tesei. Only the third pair, Birindelli and Paccagnini, managed to get into the harbor, but even they had no success because, after passing the boom, their "pig" also began to function badly. Birindelli made a spirited attempt to manhandle it under the battleship *Barham*, which was now within reach; but two hundred yards short of the target the torpedo sank for good. Birindelli and Paccagnini were taken prisoners. The other four pilots managed to get back to Italy, thanks to our excellent undercover organization in Spain. But Tesei's physique, already impaired by intensive underwater training and still more by his gallant rescue work in August, never fully recovered.

In his report on the Gibraltar operation Tesei makes no mention of the gruelling hours that he spent, submerged or awash, in the enemy port. His account is coldly impersonal: nothing about the efforts and frustrations of the pilots, only a technical explanation of the reasons for failure. Captain Falcomatà, however, the medical officer of the 10th Flotilla, diagnosed a cardiac lesion in Tesei and declared him "unfit for underwater operations for six months." His knowledge of this weakness led Borghese later to certain conclusions about Tesei's death; but these are not supported by the facts or anything that Tesei wrote himself.

He was certainly not a man to admit that the body could prevail over the spirit; and he gave proof of this a few days after his return from Gibraltar. He was asked by the Under Secretary at the Admiralty to apply his technical knowledge and his experience as a diver to the salvaging of the battleship *Cavour*, sunk by an air torpedo in Taranto Harbor on 11 November 1940. This was only three or four days after the medical officer had pronounced him unfit; but as soon as he was told by Admiral Cavagnari that his services were needed, he put on his diving suit and spent several days investigating the wreck of the *Cavour*. The discoveries he made during a series of long dives undoubtedly contributed much to the salvaging of the ship.

IV

To Italian seamen Malta was more than a dangerous enemy base; by implication it was a challenge. It seemed an act of historical injustice that this hostile island should exist in the middle of Mare Nostrum and on the direct route between Sicily and North Africa. Many people thought of Malta in this way;

but Tesei made an attack on the island the object of his whole life. He pondered an operation against Valletta in 1935, when he and Toschi completed their designs for the human torpedo; and his mind was still on the same subject in 1940. He continued to dream of it even when ill-health should have made him give up his work with Special Forces.

He used to say, with the conviction of one propounding a dogma, that "the world must hear of a daring attack on Malta by the Italians—the actual results are of minor importance...." And, of course, as soon as G.H.Q. decided to make such an attack, he pulled every string to get himself included in the expedition, in spite of his physical condition and the fact that Moccagatta's plans, approved by the Admiralty, provided for a surface attack by assault boats only. I must add here that this method had already been used with success at Suda Bay, where Faggioni with six assault boats, carried by the destroyers *Sella* and *Crispi*, had sunk the cruiser *York* and about 30,000 tons of merchant shipping. It seemed logical to try the same thing again; and, in fact, the assault boats had already made two attempts on Malta in May and June 1941. Neither had any success, but the failure, if it can be called that, had been due on one occasion to bad weather and on the other to damage to the assault boats. The third expedition was therefore organized along the same lines.

This meant that there was no part for Tesei, the underwater expert. But having set his heart on the operation for so long, he made an urgent request—more than a request perhaps—to take part in it with his human torpedo. He encountered a certain amount of opposition at first, but had his way in the end.

I do not know whether Tesei accompanied his request with a plan for co-operation between surface and submarine craft; nor do I know what part, if any, he played in working out the plan finally used. My impression is that he did prepare an outline plan of his own, but that it was never put into practice. But this is only guesswork, for it is notoriously difficult to reconstruct any operation after the event from the surviving records, diaries and reports. The only thing one can say for certain is that the whole affair turned out to be far more complicated than the previous operation at Suda Bay or *Scirè's* two expeditions against Gibraltar and Alexandria.

V

The assault force which sailed from Augusta on the evening of 25 July 1941 was organized as follows:

The fast tender *Diana,* with nine assault boats on board, towing a special motor boat on which two "pigs" were embarked.

MAS 452 with Moccagatta, the force commander, on board.

MAS 451, towing a fast motorboat, from which Lt. Cdr. Giobbe would later direct the surface attack.

This list gives some idea of the complicated task force which had to be set in motion that night. It was essential to the success of the operation that each move should interlock with the next according to an exact timetable. The vital point was the cutting of the net below the bridge between Fort Sant'Elmo and Valletta. It was through this gap that the assault boats were to make their way into the harbor; and the passage had to be cleared before dawn at 4:30 a.m., because there could be no question of carrying out the surface attack by daylight.

Everything depended, therefore, on the cutting of the net; and it was natural that this job should go to Tesei in view of his known courage and experience. He was to take one of the "pigs" with Pedretti as his number two. The other, crewed by Lt. Costa and the diver Barla, was to enter Marsu Mascetto Creek independently to attack the submarines moored there. The nine assault boats were to enter the Grand Harbor through the gap in the net blown by Tesei, having been guided as far as the entrance by Giobbe in the fast motorboat.

Up to a certain point this plan worked well. The first hitch occurred about fifteen miles from Malta, where the MAS, the assault boats and the two motor boats were to part company from *Diana* and proceed independently. It was midnight when this mishap took place, which would ordinarily have been of no importance, but now had the serious result of delaying the whole underwater contingent. *MAS 451*, which had taken in tow the motorboat with the "pigs" on board, fouled her screw and collided with the tow astern. It would not have been worth mentioning but for the fact that it took the MAS more than an hour to clear the screw and get under way again. This lost

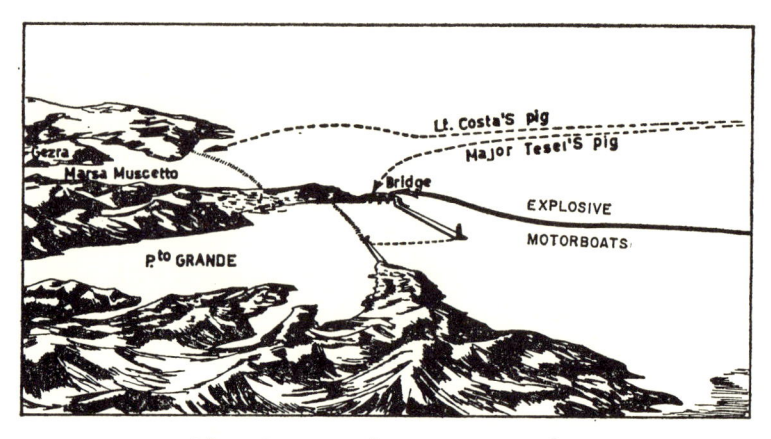

Plan for assault against Malta.

hour, by delaying Tesei's attack, sealed the fate of the whole operation.

Costa, the pilot of the second "pig," who was also in charge of the motorboat, gave this account after his release: "We were towed to within five miles of Valletta, where *MAS 451* cast off the line and stood by. At 2 a.m. I began my run in. As we had lost so much time, I approached at a much higher speed than had been planned. Nevertheless, we were able to get within 1,200 yards of the Sant'Elmo bridge without being detected. It was then about 3 a.m. We stopped and Tesei and I launched the 'pigs.' His was riding normally, but mine, probably as the result of the earlier collision, was noticeably down by the stern."

By 3 a.m., therefore, the motorboat was within 1,200 yards of the target; but by the time the "pigs" had been launched and the trim of Costa's craft corrected, another forty-five minutes had passed. It was not until 3:45 that Tesei, now a good deal behind schedule, could start moving towards the Sant'-Elmo bridge. The delay was not his fault; on the contrary, he, Costa and the other two had done everything possible to make up time. It was simply one of those hazards which always accompany an operation of this kind.

The passage under the Sant'Elmo bridge had to be cleared by 4:30 a.m. This left Tesei only three-quarters of an hour in which to reach the net, attach the warhead of the torpedo and swim clear before the explosion. It was plainly not enough. At 3:45 Tesei could still have turned back, having decided that his part in the plan was unworkable. But that would have meant the failure of the whole operation, which Tesei was not prepared even to consider. He therefore took a far more serious but highly characteristic decision. The only witness, though a good one, is Costa, who was the last person to speak to Tesei. "The plan provided," he writes, "for the blowing of the net at 4:30 precisely. . . . Tesei said: 'I don't suppose I shall be able to do more than get there in the time. But the charge will be fired at 4:30. If necessary, I shall use an instantaneous fuse.'"

That meant the almost certain sacrifice of his life; but Tesei, with his faithful companion, Alcide Pedretti, said good-by to Costa at 3:45 a.m., having made his decision. Borghese maintains that Tesei, knowing his state of health, "gallantly threw away what was left of his life to help his comrades and in the hope of forcing a great victory. It was done deliberately." This is only true in the sense that Tesei did decide to blow himself up. But he did not make that decision until 3:45 a.m. on the morning of 26 July, and then only because it was forced on him by circumstance. If he could have done so, he would certainly have given himself a margin of safety before the explosion. Besides, there is no evidence that he ever spoke even vaguely of suicide. The letter he wrote to Carlo Matteini, before this as before his other operations, contains no hint of any such thing. It is a moving testament of faith in his dominant idea: "Dear Carlo—A final note before the big bang. If I don't come back, please put on the funeral cards 'For King and Country—Lt. Cdr. (E) Teseo Tesei—The Family.' Nothing more. This may sound silly, but I feel strongly about it. Please tell the Duke of Spoleto that I am going solely on His Majesty's Service. I don't know if we shall pull it off.' Viva il Re! Teseo."

This is not the letter of a potential suicide. Although Tesei knew what risks he was running and faced the possibility of death, it was only in the same sense that any other member of Special Forces might have done. Another argument finally rules out any question of suicide. Tesei might have decided to end his own life; but he would never have sacrificed Alcide Pedretti's. If he involved him, it can only have been because the service required it and not by his own wish.

Tesei reached the net certainly no earlier than 4:30 a.m. and perhaps a few minutes after. He then did as he had told Costa he would do—adjusted the fuse for an instantaneous explosion. We have an account of what happened from Costa: "At about 4:45," says his report, which gives the times a few minutes late throughout, "I heard the explosion. Lt. Cdr. Tesei had sacrificed himself...."

VI

We left the assault boats at midnight, at the point where they parted company from *Diana*. By two o'clock they were about two miles off Malta, grouped round Giobbe's motorboat. One of the assault boats had been damaged and was scuttled, leaving eight, piloted by Frassetto, Carabelli, Bosio, Zaniboni, Pedrini, Folliero, Marchisio and Capriotti.

These young—very young—officers and petty officers of the 10th Flotilla were calm and determined. Giobbe led them towards their objective to mark down the lie of the land. Twelve hundred yards from the harbor entrance, they waited for the explosion of Tesei's charge to give the signal that a passage had been opened through the net. Giobbe could not let them go until he was certain that the way was clear into the Grand Harbor. But meanwhile time was running on. It was close to dawn; streaks of light began to appear in the east and still there was no explosion. By 4:30 nothing had happened. They waited another three, four, five minutes, but they could not afford to lose any more time. Giobbe had to make up his mind either to call the operation off or to send in his men while the net was still uncut.

The men of Special Forces never gave up an operation until they had tried everything and Giobbe followed this tradition. He decided to send two assault boats against the net and pass the remaining six into the harbor through the gap which they had made. If Tesei and Pedretti were still at or near the net, they would inevitably be blown to pieces by the explosion; but that was a risk which Giobbe had to take. It was better to lose lives than compromise the success of the operation.

Frassetto and Carabelli were ordered to blow up the net, if it were still intact. A few seconds later the rest of the party, with Bosio leading, were to pass through into the harbor. It was almost exactly at this moment that Costa, piloting his "pig" to Marsu Mascetto Creek, heard Tesei's charge explode. So did the pilots of the assault boats; but they had received their orders, started their run, and had no choice but to carry on.

Frassetto and Carabelli headed for the net. The first, following instructions, having aimed his boat straight at the target, abandoned her about a hundred yards off. Carabelli[1] chose to remain on board, steering his frail craft to the end, so as to

[1] Sub. Lieut. Aristide Carabelli from Milan.

make certain of his target. He was killed in the subsequent explosion. On the previous evening, before the expedition sailed, he had left behind a letter for his parents: "We are going on a difficult job and the odds are against our coming back alive. I am glad of the chance to offer my life for my country and a noble cause...."

Tesei and Pedretti had already given their lives, now it was Carabelli's turn. But the sad list did not stop there. The two assault boats of Carabelli and Frassetto went up together, almost at the same time as Tesei's torpedo. The result was a formidable explosion, much more violent than had been meant. It tore the net apart; but it also brought down one of the piers of the Sant'Elmo bridge, so that one complete span fell into the sea. The gap, for which three lives had been sacrificed, was thus effectively closed by a tangle of metal half in and half out of the water.

At the same moment all the searchlights in the base came on, converging on the six assault boats as they headed for the Grand Harbor. Machine guns, Bofors and Oerlikons all opened up. In the centre of this furious cross-fire the assault boats, probably still unaware of what had happened, were dashing at full speed towards a gap which was totally obstructed. One after another they were hit and sank or caught fire. All their pilots were more or less seriously wounded. Only Bosio's boat at the head of the line was still miraculously afloat; but the rudder had jammed and she was turning in a close circle out of her pilot's control. Zaniboni, wounded and in the water, saw what was happening. He also saw that a British launch had come out of Malta in search of survivors and was heading towards Bosio. He set out laboriously to swim to the derelict assault boats in the hope of preventing her capture and rescuing the pilot. But neither he nor the launch were in time: Bosio forestalled them both by blowing up his boat. He was the fourth Italian to sacrifice himself that day rather than fail in his duty.

Zaniboni, Frassetto, Pedrini, Folliero, Marchisio and Capriotti were taken prisoners; as also was Costa after he had destroyed his torpedo.

The reaction of the defense was too quick and the fire too well synchronized to have been the result of an unexpected alarm. As we now know, the alert had been given before either Tesei's or Carabelli's charges exploded, for the assault force had been spotted by radar at midnight and kept under close observation ever since. The searchlights, the guns and the fighters were all standing by, so that two minutes sufficed "to sweep everything out of the water."

But in fact something was still afloat not far from Malta—Giobbe's motorboat and the two MAS. The fighters threw themselves on this new target. As dawn was breaking, the Italian boats were machine gunned from deck level. One MAS caught fire and the other was hit repeatedly. Moccagatta, Giobbe, Parodi, Falcomatà, Montanari, Costantini and Zocchi were all killed. The British lost one aircraft.

So ended the attack on Malta, the most daring and complex operation carried out by our Special Forces. It was brought to a tragic end by a combination of bad luck and unexpected difficulties; but there was, perhaps, no other operation which so well displayed the courage and patriotism of Italian seamen.

XXIV

Olterra's Commander

OLTERRA was Visintini's masterpiece. The original idea of turning an old tub at Algeciras into a special instrument of war was not his alone; but it was he who transformed the battered tanker into a jumping-off base, entirely unsuspected by the British, for the assault forces which were to operate against Gibraltar.

He set up a workshop in the ship's hold and a sort of wetdock from which to launch the "pigs"; he organized a continuous watch on shipping in the British port, and directed and inspired the men of the Special Force—*Ursa Major* as it was later called—which was to attack the British Mediterranean stronghold.

Visintini was quite at home at Gibraltar. He had been there on the night of 26 May 1941, and again the following September, in the submarine *Sciré* under the command of Borghese, who moved about in the Straits during the war as freely as if he were on maneuvres off Spezia. Visintini's visits to Gibraltar, before he settled down on the salvaged tanker at Algeciras, had, of course, taken place at night and had been confined to the waters of the harbor; he had not set foot on the quay or in the streets of the fortress. On the first occasion they had set out to attack merchant ships in the harbor, but, although Visintini reached the ship he was to mine, the attack was a failure. The second attempt was more successful, because they not only sank and damaged some ships, but Visintini and his second got right into the inner basin, as Birindelli had done in the unfortunate expedition of October 1940.

Visintini penetrated the inner basin once more, in December 1942, but this time, as we shall see, it cost him his life, and in spite of many determined attempts no Italian ever got in again. I do not wish to detract in any way from the courage or the ability of the later frogmen who were among the most experienced in the Navy, but mention it in order to emphasize how difficult it was for them to pierce the triple line of nets, even when they and their torpedoes were launched from *Sciré* close by, below the mouth of the Guadarranque.

After his failure in May 1941 Visintini made his second and successful attempt on 20 September that year. Three pairs of frogmen were launched by *Sciré*, two of which attached their torpedoes to tankers in the main anchorage. The third pair, Visintini and Magro, made straight for the fleet anhcorage. They outwitted the guard boats and the depth charges exploding round them (a new departure, this), eluded the sentries and searchlights and got over the nets and steel cables barring the entrance. It was a terrible risk; but anchored inside were the battleship *Nelson*, the aircraft carrier *Ark Royal*, a couple of cruisers, many destroyers and some tankers—all targets well worth the risk.

Once inside, Visintini consulted the luminous dial of his wristwatch. It was five past four; it had taken him nearly four hours to cover about three sea miles and penetrate the port defences. He surfaced at once to reconnoitre the possibilities left him in the limited time available. The major targets, *Ark Royal* and *Nelson*, were moored too far down the bay, so he had to choose between the cruiser *Leander*, anchored near him, and a big tanker lying alongside the Detached Mole. He headed for the tanker, in the hope that her considerable cargo of oil would catch fire when she blew up and damage *Leander*, *Ark*

Royal, *Nelson* and other ships as well. This proved a false hope, for the oil did not catch fire, any more than it did in the tanker mined by Martellotto two months later at Alexandria. It would appear from this that the fuel oil used by the British was much less inflammable than we had supposed.

Visintini and Magro, having left their little present of 600-lbs of explosive in the belly of the tanker *Derbydale*, succeeded in making their way out of the harbor and landed on the Spanish coast at 6:30 a.m. after six and a half hours in the water. *Derbydale* blew up at 8:45 a.m. at about the same time as the tankers *Durham* and *Fiona Shell* in the outer harbor, where they had been mined by the other two pairs of frogmen from *Sciré*. Precious oil tankers to the tune of thirty thousand tons were thus sunk or irreparably damaged without loss to the Italians. All the frogmen returned safely to Italy.

After two trips to Gibraltar and two arduous years with the assault forces, leading a life which necessitated the utmost physical fitness, Visintini might well have asked for leave. But he did not do so then, any more than he did at the time of his marriage to the woman he had loved for so long, or, in February 1941, when he heard that his airforce brother, Mario, had been killed in East Africa after shooting down seventeen enemy aircraft. On this occasion, his commanding officer had offered him an alternative assignment, as he was now the sole support of his widowed mother; but Visintini replied that the death of his brother, posthumously awarded the Gold Cross, was an added inducement to him to carry out his own duty right to the end.

It was, in fact, after his brother's death that the two Gibraltar expeditions took place and it seems almost as if the figures of his brother and of his father, that great Istrian patriot, upheld him and inspired him to ever greater daring. In November 1941, he wrote to his fiancée: "I know that they can hear me and are proud of me, as I am of them, even to tears. Our family history is coming to an end, because everything has been given to Italy. . . . We talk and smile, secure in the knowledge that the Great Ones are guiding us."

He served with me in *Torelli* on an Atlantic patrol in September 1940, and I remember clearly his seriousness, his dedicated purpose, his professional skill and his indomitable spirit. Before joining *Torelli* he had asked to be transferred to the underwater assault forces. At Bordeaux, when we arrived there with the submarine, he received the news that his application had been granted; he left at once for Spezia and at the base on the Serchio he lived with Tesei, Toschi, de La Penne and Marceglia. With these four, later so distinguished, he completed his training on S.L.C.s.

After the second attack on Gibraltar, Visintini might well have sat back. But he was not satisfied. Perhaps he was still dreaming of those big British ships anchored at the far end of the bay just out of his reach. So, in the winter of 1942, he started an impressively realistic training of new frogmen and by the following summer he was in Spain getting *Olterra* ready.

Full details of the transformation of *Olterra* have already appeared in the works of Cappellini, Borghese and Spigai, and also in Italian and foreign newspapers and reviews. So I will not give a technical account here of how *Olterra* was fitted out or the frogmen and their torpedoes launched. What is, however, less well-known is Visintini's diary, in which he recorded all his thoughts throughout the war. In it we read, pencilled in his small, firm handwriting, a lively account of his day's work; his operational notes—observations on the defense of Gibraltar, the movements of ships in the harbor, the people he had met in the course of his work or whom he had seen near *Olterra*. Mixed up with this was everything he would have liked to say to Maria, his wife whom he had married a few days before leaving Italy, and whose love for him had grown to an almost mystical devotion.

I have seen few documents so full of poetry. It is a pity that those who put the exploits of our Special Forces on the screen, did not think to draw on it, when they wanted a contrast with the action-sequences, instead of introducing belly dancers and slinky adventuresses.

But we must now come back to *Olterra*, which was very soon in operation. By the late summer of 1942, Visintini was able to put up to the 10th Flotilla his own plan for the employment of the pilots assigned to or earmarked for the tanker. It was a simple plan, which can be summarized as follows:

(1) Nothing was to be done until a large warship entered Gibraltar, the waiting period being employed to make a minute study of the enemy's defensive measures;

(2) As soon as the big ships arrived, they were to be attacked at once by three "pigs."

It will be noted that Visintini did not even consider using *Olterra* to attack the cargo boats berthed in the merchant ship anchorage outside the boom, which was also carefully patrolled. His aim was bolder and more ambitious.

You must remember that it was now well on in 1942. England had suffered losses at Suda Bay and in Alexandria; she had also seen a big tanker blow up in Gibraltar itself. Her defensive measures were therefore at a maximum. The boom nets had been multiplied and an almost uninterrupted mine-barrage laid across the mouth of the harbor. But there are no obstacles for a daring man. Visintini had put up an audacious plan and, when it was approved, set about executing it with a careful attention to detail, which was remarkable in a young man of twenty-seven. He prepared his men and his weapons, studied the set of the currents and perfected his knowledge of the defenses, observing the searchlights, gun boats, patrols and submarine mines. Then he sat down to wait for the British Navy.

He did not have to wait very long. On 6 December the battle-

Olterra's *Commander*

ships *Nelson* and *Renown* entered the harbor with the aircraft carriers *Furious* and *Formidable* and a number of smaller ships. Activity round the boom was intensified. The little guard boats bustled about; searchlights lit up the harbor almost continuously; and automatic mines went off every three minutes. Across the entrance to the naval basin, the explosions were almost continuous. Nevertheless, on the night of the 7th the men from *Olterra* came out from their base to attack the enemy. Visintini allocated the targets as follows: for himself and Magro, the battleship *Nelson;* for Cella and Leone, the aircraft carrier *Furious;* for Manisco and Varini, the aircraft carrier *Formidable*.

To reach their objectives they had to find a way into the naval basin, running the gauntlet of guard boats, searchlights and patrols; break through the nets and get across the mined area. But, as Visintini wrote in his diary: "Nothing but death can stop us." He went into the attack without hesitation and, according to a British account, did in fact succeed in getting right into the naval basin.

This report says: "At 2:15 a.m. on 8 December three assault craft carrying two men each tried to enter Gibraltar harbor. One was seen by a sentry, illuminated and then attacked and sunk by gunfire and depth charges. The crew were picked up by a merchant ship. It is thought that they had been brought from Italy by the submarine *Ambra*. A second pair got into the naval basin, but were destroyed by depth charges, while a third pair is thought to have died before reaching the basin."

It is not true, as we know, that the attackers had been launched from a submarine. (The mistake shows how well the secret of *Olterra* had been kept.) It is also partly untrue to say that the third pair died before reaching the harbor. In fact, though Leone disappeared, Cella was able to return to *Olterra*. On the other hand it is true that one pair—Visintini and Magro —succeeded in getting inside the naval basin. Having done so, they were killed in the mine belt into which they had boldly plunged.

The bodies of Visintini and Magro came to the surface inside the harbor a few days later. They were buried at sea with full military honors; and a wreath was contributed by Lts. Crabbe and Bayley of the Gibraltar security force.

APPENDIX

ITALIAN SUBMARINES IN THE ATLANTIC

SUBMARINE	COMMANDING OFFICER*	REMARKS
FINZI	Dominici	Later under command of Giudice. Disarmed at Bordeaux at the Armistice.
TAZZOLI	Raccanelli	Under command of Fecia di Cossato, sank 100,000 tons of enemy shipping. Under command of Caito disappeared without trace.
CALVI	Caridi	Under command of Longobardo was sunk by corvette *Lulworth* 14 July 1942.
TORELLI	Cocchia	Later commanded by Longobardo. Turned over, under command of Groppallo, to transport for Far East; was captured by the Germans at the Armistice.
MALASPINA	Leoni	Disappeared without trace while under the command of Prini.
BIANCHI	Giovannini	Later under command of Tosoni. Sunk by submarine *Severn* on 7 August 1941.
BARACCA	Bertarelli	Sunk by *Croome*, 8 September 1941, while under command of Viani.
FAA' DI BRUNO	Enrici	Sunk by destroyer *Havelock*, 8 November 1940.
CAPPELLINI	Todaro	First mission—to Ceuta—under Masi; after Todaro, passed to Ravedin and then to Auconi, under whom eventually turned over to Far East transport. Captured by the Germans at the Armistice.
VENIERO	Petroni	First passage, submerged, under command of Buonamici. Repatriated August 1941 and sunk from the air south of the Balearics, under command of Zappetta.
MOCENIGO	Agostini	Repatriated August 1941. Sunk by aircraft at Cagliari 13 May 1943.
GLAUCO	Mellina	Under command of Baroni, was sunk by *Wishart* 27 June 1941.
OTARIA	Vocaturo	Repatriated August 1941.
BRIN	Longanesi	Ditto.

* At time of original transit through the Straits of Gibraltar.

SUBMARINE	COMMANDING OFFICER	REMARKS
TARANTINI	Iaschi	Sunk 15 December 1940 by submarine *Thunderbolt*.
GIULIANI	D'Elia	Turned over, under the command of Tei, to Far East transport. Captured at Singapore.
BAGNOLINI	Tosoni Pittoni	Disarmed at Bordeaux at the Armistice.
MARCONI	Chialamberto	Disappeared without trace.
DA VINCI	Calda	Later commanded by Gazzana who sank 60,000 tons of enemy shipping in one mission. Sunk by English destroyers while returning to base 23 May 1943.
EMO	Liannazza	Repatriated. Sunk 10 November 1942 by destroyer *Lord Nuffield* off Algiers. C.O. Franco.
MOROSINI	Criscuolo	Disappeared without trace 8 August 1942. C.O. D'Alessendro.
NANI	Polizzi	Sunk 7 January 1941 by the corvette *Anemone*.
MARCELLO	Teppati	Sunk by aircraft 6 February 1941.
BARBARIGO	Chiglieri	Later commanded by Grossi. Sunk without trace while under command of De Julio.
DANDOLO	Boris	Repatriated in summer of 1941.
ARGO	Crepas	Repatriated and scuttled at the Armistice.
VELELLA	Terra	Repatriated. Sunk 7 September 1943 by the submarine *Shakespeare*.
ARCHIMEDE	Spagone	Arrived from Massawa. Sunk from the air 15 April 1943 on the coast of Brazil. C.O. Saccardo.
FERRARIS	Piomarta	Arrived from Massawa. Sunk after surface battle with destroyer *Lamerton* 25 October 1941.
GUGLIELMOTTI	Salvatori	Repatriated from Massawa. Sunk by submarine *Unbeaten* 17 March 1942. C.O. Tamburini.
PERLA	Nappi	Repatriated from Massawa. Lost 9 July 1942 off the Syrian coast. C.O. Ventura.
CAGNI	Liannazza	Completed profitable mission under Roselli. Repatriated after the Armistice through Suez.

NAVIES AND MEN

An Arno Press Collection

Bragadin, Marc' Antonio. **The Italian Navy in World War II.** 1957
Bunker, John Gorley. **Liberty Ships.** 1972
Cagle, Malcolm W., and Frank A. Manson. **The Sea War in Korea.** 1957
Chatterton, E. Keble. **Q-Ships and Their Story.** 1972
Cocchia, Aldo. **The Hunters and the Hunted.** 1958
Cohen, Philip M. **Bathymetric Navigation and Charting.** 1970
Frost, Holloway H. **The Battle of Jutland.** 1964
Gray, J.A.C. **Amerika Samoa.** 1960
Johnson, Robert Erwin. **Rear Admiral John Rodgers.** 1967
Johnson, Robert Erwin. **Thence Round Cape Horn.** 1963
Keeler, William Frederick. **Aboard the USS Florida: 1863-65.** 1968
Lewis, Charles Lee. **Admiral De Grasse and American Independence.** 1945
Lewis, Charles Lee. **David Glasgow Farragut: Admiral in the Making.** 1941
Lewis, Charles Lee. **David Glasgow Farragut: Our First Admiral.** 1943
Lewis, Charles Lee. **Matthew Fontaine Maury.** 1927
McKee, Christopher. **Edward Preble.** 1972
Milligan, John D. **Gunboats Down the Mississippi.** 1965
Morris, Richard Knowles. **John P. Holland.** 1966
Paullin, Charles Oscar. **Commodore John Rodgers.** 1967
Raeder, Erich. **My Life.** 1960
Ransom, M.A., with Eloise Katherine Engle. **Sea of the Bear.** 1964.
Sloan, Edward William, III. **Benjamin Franklin Isherwood, Naval Engineer.** 1965
Swann, Leonard Alexander, Jr. **John Roach, Maritime Entrepreneur.** 1965
Thomas, Walter "R." **From a Small Naval Observatory.** 1972
Willoughby, Malcolm F. **The U.S. Coast Guard in World War II.** 1957